cc.
2001
Mark —
for all the fish
you catch! Renny

CLASSIC
FISH
COOKING

CLASSIC
FISH
COOKING

DELICIOUS DISHES FOR
ALL OCCASIONS

Linda Doeser

Sebastian Kelly

First published in 1999 by Sebastian Kelly

© Anness Publishing Limited 1999

Produced by Anness Publishing Limited
Hermes House, 88–89 Blackfriars Road
London SE1 8HA

ISBN 1 84081 262 1

Publisher: Joanna Lorenz
Copy Editor: Leslie Viney
Designer: Mason Linklater
Illustrations: Madeleine David

Front cover: Lisa Tai, Designer; Thomas Odulate, Photographer;
Helen Trent, Stylist; Joy Skipper, Home Economist

Recipes: Catherine Atkinson, Alex Barker, Ruby Le Bois, Carla Capalbo,
Maxine Clark, Christine France, Carole Handslip, Sarah Gates, Shirley Gill,
Norma MacMillan, Sue Maggs, Katherine Richmond, Jenny Stacey, Liz Trigg, Hilaire Walden,
Lara Washburn, Steven Wheeler
Photographers: Karl Adamson, Edward Allwright, Steve Baxter, James Duncan, John Freeman,
Michelle Garrett, Amanda Heywood, Don Last

Previously published as part of a larger compendium, *The Great Fish & Shellfish Cookbook*

Printed in Hong Kong/China

1 3 5 7 9 10 8 6 4 2

NOTES
Standard spoon and cup measurements are level.

Medium eggs should be used unless otherwise stated.

CONTENTS

Introduction

The variety of fish and shellfish is almost endless and, as fish combines superbly with just about every other imaginable ingredient, the choice of classic dishes is almost bewildering. This mouthwatering collection has been inspired by great fish dishes from all over the world—French Bouillabaisse, Italian Roast Sea Bass, Russian Salmon Coulibiac, Turkish Cold Fish, Indian Fish Stew, Louisiana Seafood Gumbo, Chinese Seafood Chow Mein and Spanish Seafood Paella, to name only some.

While some recipes are elaborate or even expensive, many of the best classic fish dishes are astonishingly simple and economical, taking full advantage of the natural flavors and textures of the ingredients. An additional benefit is the high nutritional value of fish. It is packed with protein, vitamins and minerals and is thought to help lower blood cholesterol levels. What is more, fish and shellfish are best cooked quickly, so even pies and casseroles take relatively little time.

An information-packed introduction provides step-by-step instructions for skinning and filleting fish and preparing shellfish, as well as making fish stock. The recipes are divided into five chapters— Soups & Appetizers, Pies & Baked Dishes, Fried & Broiled Dishes, Casseroles & Stews, and Pasta, Noodle & Rice Dishes. Each one incorporates a wide variety of types from cod to salmon and from scallops to squid. Hints and tips throughout the book provide additional advice on alternative ingredients and techniques.

Boning Round Fish for Stuffing

1 Gut the fish through the stomach as described on the previous page.

2 Slit the fish on either side of the backbone, cutting the flesh away from the bone until it is completely detached.

3 With a heavy pair of scissors, snip the backbone once at the head and once at the tail.

4 Carefully lift out the backbone and discard.

Boning a Round Fish Through the Stomach

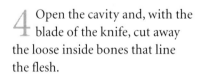

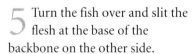

1 Gut the fish through the stomach as previously described. Continue the stomach slit on one side of the backbone as far as the tail.

2 Open the cavity and remove the insides.

3 Clean the insides of the fish, wiping away any remaining blood or guts.

4 Open the cavity and, with the blade of the knife, cut away the loose inside bones that line the flesh.

5 Turn the fish over and slit the flesh at the base of the backbone on the other side.

6 With the blade of the knife, cut loose the inside bones lining the flesh in the same way as the first side.

7 Carefully loosen the backbone of the fish completely.

8 With scissors, snip the backbone at the head and the tail.

9 Carefully peel the backbone away from the flesh with any inside bones.

10 The head can be kept and the two side fillets rolled in spirals, skin side inward. Alternatively, fold the skin outward and tuck the tail inside.

11 Alternatively, the head and skin can be removed and the fillets rolled or cooked flat.

Cutting Steaks and Cutlets

1 With a large, sharp knife, slice the fish across, at a right angle to the backbone, into slices of the desired thickness.

2 If necessary, cut through the backbone with kitchen scissors or a knife with a serrated blade.

COOK'S TIP

Round fish and large flat fish, such as halibut, are often cut into steaks and cutlets for cooking. Steaks are cut from the tail end of the fish, while cutlets are cut from the center. They are usually cut about 1–1½ inches thick.

Filleting Round Fish

1 Holding the knife horizontally, slit the skin from head to tail along one side of the backbone.

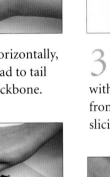

2 Cut down to the backbone just behind the fish's head.

3 Holding the knife flat and keeping the blade in contact with the bone, cut off the flesh from head to tail in a continuous slicing motion.

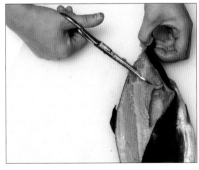

4 Cut the backbone at the tail end with scissors.

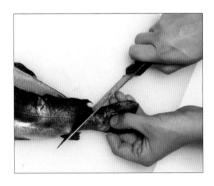

5 Trim off the tail.

6 Cut the fish into two fillets.

Skinning a Fillet

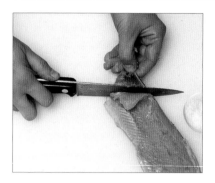

1 Secure the fillet with salt on a cutting board. Insert a sharp, flexible knife at the end of the fillet and hold securely.

2 Working in a cutting motion against the skin, move the knife along the fillet.

3 Continue until the skin has been completely removed from the flesh.

Boning Flat Fish

1 Using a flexible knife, cut along the backbone.

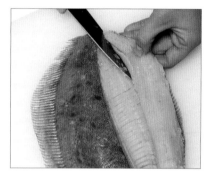

3 Cut to the edge of the transverse bones, but do not remove the fillet completely.

7 Loosen the bones from the flesh of the fish.

2 Cut the flesh away from the bones, holding the knife almost parallel to them.

4 Turn the fish over and repeat for the opposite fillet.

5 Fold both fillets out.

6 Using a strong pair of scissors, cut the bones along the edges.

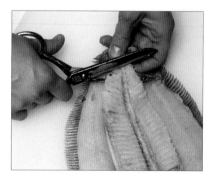

8 With kitchen scissors, snip the backbone at both the head and the tail ends.

9 Lift the backbone at the tail end and pull, stripping it from the flesh underneath.

Filleting Flat Fish

3 Turn the fish over and cut a straight line from the tail to the head as before.

4 Work the flesh away from the bones as described in steps 1 and 2, and then repeat with the fourth fillet.

1 With a sharp knife, cut around the edge of the fish to outline the shape of the fillets. Cut a straight line from the tail to the head along the spine through the bone. Keeping the knife almost flat, slip it between the flesh and the rib bones.

2 Cut away the fillet, using a stroking motion and keeping the knife flat. Continue cutting until the fillet and flesh against the fins has been detached with the skin in one piece. Continue with the other fillet.

Skinning Flat Fish

1 Lay the fish on a cutting board, with the dark side on top. With a sharp knife held at an angle, cut across the skin where the tail joins the body, taking care not to cut all the way through.

2 With the knife still held at an angle, start to cut. Keep the fish secure on the board with some salt and gradually pry the flap of skin away from the flesh. When you have a good flap of skin, grasp it with one hand and hold the other end of the fish with your other hand. Firmly pull the skin toward the head.

Fish Stock

1½ pounds heads, bones and trimmings
   from white fish

1 onion, sliced

2 celery stalks with leaves, chopped

1 carrot, sliced

½ lemon, sliced (optional)

1 bay leaf

3–4 fresh parsley sprigs

6 black peppercorns

5½ cups water

½ cup dry white wine

1 Rinse the fish heads, bones and trimmings under cold running water. Put them in a large saucepan with the vegetables, lemon, if using, herbs, peppercorns, water and wine. Bring to a boil, skimming the surface frequently. Reduce the heat and simmer for 25 minutes.

2 Strain the stock, but do not press down on the contents of the strainer. If you are not using the stock immediately, let cool and then refrigerate. Fish stock should be used within 2 days. It may be frozen and kept for up to 3 months.

Preparing Mussels and Clams

Mollusks, such as mussels and clams, should be eaten very fresh and should be alive when you buy and cook them (unless they have been shelled and frozen or are canned). You can tell if they are alive because their shells are tightly closed. Any that are open should shut immediately when tapped sharply with a knife. Any that do not close or that have broken shells should be discarded.

If you have collected the shellfish yourself, let them stand in a bucket of sea water for several hours, changing the water once or twice. Do not use fresh water, as it will kill them. Add one or two handfuls of cornmeal or flour to the water to help clean the stomachs of the shellfish. Shellfish bought from a shop will already have been purged of sand.

1 Scrub the shells with a stiff brush and rinse well. This can be done under cold running water.

2 Pull off the "beards" (their anchor threads) with the help of a small knife. Rinse well.

3 To steam, put a little dry white wine or water in a large saucepan, together with any flavorings specified in the recipe. Add the mussels or clams, cover tightly and bring to a boil. Cook for 5–10 minutes or until the shells open, shaking the pan from time to time. Discard any that do not open.

4 Serve the shellfish in their shells or shell them before using. Strain the cooking liquid, which includes the liquid from the shells, and spoon it over the shellfish or use it as the basis for a seafood sauce.

5 To open a live clam or mussel, hold it in one hand with the hinge in your palm. Insert the side of a clam or oyster knife blade between the shell halves and work it around to cut through the hinge muscle.

6 Open the shell and cut the clam or mussel out of the shell. Do this over a bowl to catch all the liquid from the shell.

Opening and Cleaning Scallops

1 To open the shell, hold the scallop with the flat shell on top. Probe between the shells with a short knife to find a small opening. Insert the blade and run it across the roof of the shell.

2 Separate the two halves of the shell, and pull apart.

3 Slide the blade under the grayish outer rim of the flesh, called the skirt, to free the scallop. Pull off the muscle with a small knife. Use the trimmed scallop, whole or halved, for cooking.

Opening Oysters

  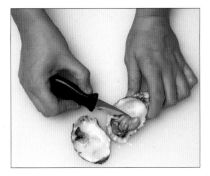

1 Place the oyster, wrapped in a clean napkin or dish towel, on a firm surface with the flatter shell on top and the hinge toward you. Holding the oyster with one hand, insert the tip of an oyster knife into the gap in the hinge.

2 Twist the blade to snap the shells apart.

3 Continue to hold the oyster firmly in the cloth and slide the blade along the inside of the upper shell to sever the muscle that holds the shell together. Discard the top shell and lift the lower, rounded shell off the napkin, making sure the liquid in it does not spill. Clean any bits of broken shell with the point of the knife.

4 Grip the lower shell firmly with your fingers. Cutting toward yourself, run the blade under the oyster to sever the muscle attaching it to the lower shell and free it.

Preparing and Deveining Shrimp

Shrimp may be cooked in their shells, but are often peeled first. The shells can be used to make an aromatic stock. The intestinal vein that runs down the back is usually removed from large shrimp, mainly because of its appearance, but also because it may contain grit that makes it unpleasant to eat. Shrimp may be sold with the heads on. These are easily pulled off with the fingers and will enhance the flavor of stock made with their shells.

1 Holding the shrimp firmly in one hand, pull off the legs with the fingers of the other hand.

2 Peel the shell away from the body. When you reach the tail, hold the body and pull away the tail; the shell will come off with it. Alternatively, you can leave the tail on the shrimp and just remove the body shell.

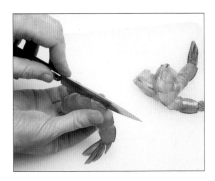 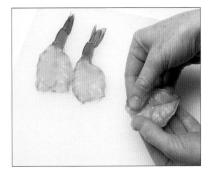

3 Make a shallow cut down the center of the curved back of the shrimp. Pull out the black vein with a toothpick or your fingers.

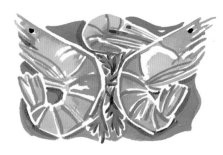

4 To make butterfly shrimp, cut along the deveining slit to split open the shrimp, without cutting all the way through. Open up the shrimp flat.

5 To devein shrimp in their shells, insert a toothpick horizontally in several places along the back where the shell overlaps to lift out the vein.

SOUPS &
APPETIZERS

Classic Italian Fish Soup

Liguria, Italy, is famous for its fish soups. In this one the fish are cooked in a broth with vegetables and then puréed. This soup can also be used to dress pasta.

Serves 6

2¼ pounds mixed fish or fish pieces, such as whiting, red mullet, pollack or cod

6 tablespoons olive oil, plus extra to serve

1 medium onion, finely chopped

1 stalk celery, chopped

1 carrot, chopped

¼ cup chopped fresh parsley

¾ cup dry white wine

3 medium tomatoes, skinned, seeded and chopped

2 garlic cloves, finely chopped

6 cups boiling water

salt and freshly ground black pepper

rounds of French bread, to serve

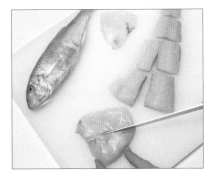

1 Scale and clean the fish, discarding all the innards, but leaving the heads on. Cut into large pieces. Rinse well in cool water.

2 Heat the oil in a large saucepan and add the onion. Cook over low to medium heat until it begins to soften. Stir in the celery and carrot, and cook for 5 more minutes. Add the parsley.

3 Pour in the wine, raise the heat, and cook until it reduces by about half. Stir in the tomatoes and garlic. Cook for 3–4 minutes, stirring occasionally. Pour in the boiling water, and bring back to a boil. Cook over medium heat for 15 minutes.

4 Stir in the fish, and simmer for 10–15 minutes or until the fish are tender. Season with salt and pepper.

5 Remove the fish from the soup with a slotted spoon. Discard the heads and any bones. Purée in a food processor. Taste for seasoning. If the soup is too thick, add a little more water.

6 To serve, heat the soup to simmering. Toast the rounds of French bread, and sprinkle with olive oil. Place 2 or 3 in the base of each soup plate before pouring over the soup.

Smoked Haddock and Potato Soup

The traditional name for this soup is "cullen skink." A cullen is the "sea town" or port district of a town, while "skink" means stock or broth.

INGREDIENTS

Serves 6

1 finnan haddock, about 12 ounces

1 onion, chopped

bouquet garni

4 cups water

1¼ pounds potatoes, quartered

2½ cups milk

2 tablespoons butter

salt and freshly ground black pepper

snipped chives, to garnish

1 Put the haddock, onion, bouquet garni and water into a large saucepan and bring to a boil. Skim the scum from the surface, then cover the pan. Reduce the heat and poach for 10–15 minutes, until the haddock flakes easily.

> ### COOK'S TIP
> ❧
> Finnan haddock is a small, whole fish that has been soaked in brine and then cold smoked.

2 Lift the haddock from the pan, using a fish server, and remove the skin and bones. Flake the flesh and reserve. Return the skin and bones to the pan and simmer, uncovered, for 30 minutes.

3 Strain the fish stock and return to the pan, then add the potatoes and simmer for about 25 minutes, or until tender. Remove the potatoes from the pan using a slotted spoon. Add the milk to the pan and bring to a boil.

4 Meanwhile, mash the potatoes with the butter, then whisk into the milk in the pan until thick and creamy. Add the flaked fish to the pan and adjust the seasoning. Sprinkle with chives and serve immediately with crusty bread.

Corn and Scallop Chowder

Fresh ears of corn are ideal for this chowder, although canned or frozen corn also works well. This soup makes a perfect lunch dish.

Serves 4–6

2 ears of corn or 1 cup frozen or
    canned corn

2½ cups milk

1 tablespoon butter or margarine

1 small leek or onion, chopped

1 small garlic clove, crushed

4 strips bacon, finely chopped

1 small green bell pepper, seeded
    and diced

1 celery stalk, chopped

1 medium potato, diced

1 tablespoon flour

1¼ cups chicken or vegetable stock

4 scallops

4 ounces cooked fresh mussels

pinch of paprika

⅔ cup light cream or half-and-half
    (optional)

salt and freshly ground black pepper

1 Using a sharp knife, slice down the ears of the corn to remove the kernels. Place half of the kernels in a food processor or blender and process with a little of the milk.

2 Melt the butter in a large saucepan and gently fry the leek or onion, garlic and bacon for 4–5 minutes, until the leek is soft but not browned. Add the diced green pepper, chopped celery and diced potato and sweat over low heat for another 3–4 minutes, stirring frequently.

3 Stir in the flour and cook for 1–2 minutes, until the mixture is golden and frothy. Gradually stir in the milk and corn mixture, stock, the remaining milk and corn kernels and seasoning.

4 Bring to a boil, then reduce the heat and simmer, partially covered, for 15–20 minutes, until the vegetables are tender.

5 Pull the corals away from the scallops and slice the white flesh into ¼-inch slices. Stir the scallops into the soup, cook for 4 minutes and then stir in the corals, mussels and paprika. Heat through for a few minutes and then stir in the cream, if using. Adjust the seasoning to taste and serve.

Bouillabaisse

Perhaps the most famous of all Mediterranean fish soups, this recipe, originating from Marseilles in the south of France, is a rich and colorful mixture of fish and shellfish, flavored with tomatoes, saffron, orange and Pernod.

INGREDIENTS

Serves 4–6

3–3½ pounds mixed fish and raw shellfish, such as red mullet, monkfish, red snapper, large raw shrimp and clams

8–10 ripe tomatoes

pinch of saffron strands

6 tablespoons olive oil

1 onion, sliced

1 leek, sliced

1 celery stalk, sliced

2 garlic cloves, crushed

1 bouquet garni

1 strip orange rind

½ teaspoon fennel seeds

1 tablespoon tomato paste

2 teaspoons Pernod

salt and freshly ground black pepper

4–6 thick slices French bread and 3 tablespoons chopped fresh parsley, to serve

1 Remove the heads, tails and fins from the fish and set the fish aside. Put the trimmings in a large pan with 5 cups water. Bring to a boil, and simmer for 15 minutes. Strain into a bowl, and reserve the liquid.

2 Cut the fish into large chunks. Leave the shellfish in their shells. Scald the tomatoes for 20 seconds, then drain and refresh in cold water. Peel and roughly chop them. Soak the saffron in 1–2 tablespoons hot water.

3 Heat the oil in a large pan, add the onion, leek and celery and cook until softened. Add the garlic, bouquet garni, orange rind, fennel seeds and tomatoes, then stir in the saffron and soaking liquid and the fish stock. Season with salt and pepper, then bring to a boil and simmer for 30–40 minutes.

4 Add the shellfish and boil for about 6 minutes. Add the fish and cook for another 6–8 minutes, until it flakes easily.

5 Using a slotted spoon, transfer the fish to a warmed serving platter. Keep the liquid boiling, to allow the oil to emulsify with the broth. Add the tomato paste and Pernod, then check the seasoning. To serve, place a slice of French bread in the base of each soup bowl, pour the broth on top and serve the fish separately, sprinkled with the parsley.

COOK'S TIP

Saffron comes from the orange and red stigmas of a type of crocus. These must be harvested by hand and it requires about 250,000 crocus flowers for a yield of 1¼ pounds of saffron. Consequently, it is extremely expensive—the highest-priced spice in the world. However, its slightly bitter flavor and pleasantly sweet aroma are unique and cannot be replaced by any other spice. It is an essential ingredient in all traditional versions of bouillabaisse and should not be omitted.

Shrimp Bisque

*The classic French method for
making a bisque requires pushing
the shellfish through a tamis, or
drum sieve. This is much simpler
and the result is just as smooth.*

INGREDIENTS

Serves 6–8

1½ pounds small or medium cooked
   shrimp in the shell
1½ tablespoons vegetable oil
2 onions, halved and sliced
1 large carrot, sliced
2 celery stalks, sliced
8 cups water
a few drops of lemon juice
2 tablespoons tomato paste
bouquet garni
2 tablespoons butter
¼ cup flour
3–4 tablespoons brandy
⅔ cup whipping cream
salt and freshly ground white pepper
flat leaf parsley sprig, to garnish

1 Remove the heads and peel off
the shells from the shrimp,
reserving them for the stock. Chill
the shrimp.

2 Heat the oil in a large pan, add
the shrimp heads and shells
and cook over high heat, stirring
frequently, until they start to
brown. Reduce the heat to
medium, add the onions, carrot
and celery and fry gently, stirring
occasionally, for about 5 minutes,
until the onions start to soften.

3 Add the water, lemon juice,
tomato paste and bouquet
garni. Bring the stock to a boil,
then reduce the heat, cover and
simmer gently for 25 minutes.
Strain the stock through a sieve.

4 Melt the butter in a heavy
saucepan over medium heat.
Stir in the flour and cook until just
golden, stirring occasionally. Add
the brandy and gradually pour in
about half of the shrimp stock,
whisking vigorously until smooth,
then whisk in the remaining
liquid. Season to taste. Reduce the
heat, cover and simmer for 5
minutes, stirring frequently.

5 Strain the soup into a clean
saucepan. Add the cream and a
little extra lemon juice to taste, if
desired, then stir in most of the
reserved shrimp and cook over
medium heat until hot. Serve
immediately, garnished with the
remaining shrimp and parsley.

Hot-and-sour Shrimp Soup

How hot this soup is depends on the type of chili used. Try tiny Thai chilies if you really want to go for the burn.

INGREDIENTS

Serves 6

8 ounces raw shrimp

2 lemon grass stalks

6¼ cups vegetable stock

4 kaffir lime leaves

2 slices peeled fresh ginger root

4 tablespoons Thai fish sauce

4 tablespoons fresh lime juice

2 garlic cloves, crushed

6 scallions, chopped

1 fresh red chili, seeded and cut
    into strips

generous 1½ cups oyster mushrooms,
    sliced

fresh cilantro leaves and kaffir lime slices,
    to garnish

1 Peel and devein the shrimp and set them aside. Put the shells in a large saucepan.

COOK'S TIP

Large jumbo shrimp are best for this recipe. They are sometimes available fresh, which have the best flavor, or frozen. It is important that they are not overcooked, or they will become unpleasantly tough.

2 Lightly crush the lemon grass and add the stalks to the pan, together with the vegetable stock, kaffir lime leaves and slices of ginger. Bring to a boil, lower the heat and simmer for 20 minutes.

3 Strain the stock into a clean pan, discarding the shrimp shells and flavorings. Add the fish sauce, lime juice, garlic, scallions, chili and mushrooms. Bring to a boil, lower the heat and simmer for 5 minutes. Add the shrimp and cook for 2–3 minutes. Garnish with cilantro and lime slices and serve.

Seafood Crêpes

The combination of fresh and smoked haddock imparts a wonderful flavor to the filling.

INGREDIENTS

Serves 4–6

For the crêpes

1 cup flour

pinch of salt

1 egg, plus 1 egg yolk

1¼ cups milk

1 tablespoon melted butter, plus extra for cooking

2–3 ounces Gruyère cheese, grated

curly salad greens, to serve

For the filling

8 ounces smoked haddock fillet

8 ounces fresh haddock fillet

1¼ cups milk

⅔ cup light cream or half-and-half

2 tablespoons butter

¼ cup flour

freshly grated nutmeg

2 hard-cooked eggs, shelled and chopped

salt and freshly ground black pepper

1 To make the crêpes, sift the flour and salt into a bowl. Make a well in the center and add the egg and egg yolk. Whisk the eggs, starting to incorporate some of the flour from around the edges.

2 Gradually add the milk, whisking all the time, until the batter is smooth and has the consistency of thin cream. Stir in the melted butter.

3 Heat a small crêpe pan or omelet pan until hot, then rub around the inside of the pan with a pad of paper towels dipped in melted butter.

4 Pour about 2 tablespoons of the batter into the pan, then tip the pan to coat the base evenly. Cook for about 30 seconds, until the underside of the crêpe is golden brown.

5 Flip the crêpe over and cook the other side until lightly browned. Repeat to make 12 crêpes, rubbing the pan with melted butter between cooking each crêpe. Stack the crêpes as you make them between sheets of waxed paper. Keep warm on a plate set over a pan of simmering water.

6 Put the smoked and fresh haddock fillets in a large pan. Add the milk and poach for 6–8 minutes, until just tender. Lift out the fish using a slotted spoon and, when cool enough to handle, remove the skin and any bones. Reserve the milk.

7 Pour the light cream or half-and-half into a measuring cup, then strain enough of the reserved milk into the cup to make the total quantity of 2 cups.

8 Melt the butter in a pan, stir in the flour and cook gently for 1 minute. Gradually mix in the milk mixture, stirring continuously, to make a smooth sauce. Cook for 2–3 minutes, until thickened. Season with salt, pepper and nutmeg. Roughly flake the haddock and fold into the sauce with the eggs. Let cool.

9 Divide the filling among the crêpes. Fold the sides of each crêpe into the center, then roll them up so that the filling is completely enclosed.

10 Butter four or six individual ovenproof dishes and arrange 2–3 filled crêpes in each, or butter one large dish for all the crêpes. Brush with melted butter and cook in a preheated oven at 350°F for 15 minutes. Sprinkle on the Gruyère and cook for another 5 minutes, until the crêpes are warmed through. Serve hot with a few curly salad greens.

VARIATION

For variety, add cooked, peeled shrimp, smoked mussels or cooked fresh, shelled mussels to the filling, instead of the chopped hard-cooked eggs.

Scallops Wrapped in Prosciutto

This is a delicious summer recipe for cooking on the barbecue.

INGREDIENTS

Serves 4

24 medium-size scallops, without corals,
   prepared for cooking
lemon juice
8–12 slices prosciutto
olive oil
freshly ground black pepper
lemon wedges, to serve

1 Preheat the broiler or prepare a charcoal fire. Sprinkle the scallops with lemon juice. Cut the prosciutto into long strips. Wrap one strip around each scallop. Thread them onto 8 skewers.

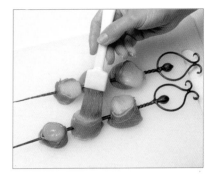

2 Brush with oil. Arrange on a baking sheet if broiling. Cook about 4 inches from the heat under a preheated broiler for 3–5 minutes on each side or until the scallops are opaque and tender. Alternatively, cook over charcoal, turning once, until the scallops are opaque and tender.

3 Set 2 skewers on each plate. Sprinkle the scallops with freshly ground black pepper and serve with lemon wedges.

COOK'S TIP

The edible parts of the scallop are the round white muscle and the coral or roe. When preparing fresh scallops, keep the skirt—the frilly part—for making stock.

Coquilles St Jacques au Gratin

This dish has been a classic on bistro menus since Hemingway's days in Paris—it makes an appealing appetizer, but could also be served as a rich and elegant main course.

INGREDIENTS

Serves 2–4

1 cup dry white wine

½ cup water

2 shallots, finely chopped

1 bay leaf

1 pound shelled scallops, rinsed

3 tablespoons butter

⅓ cup all-purpose flour

6 tablespoons whipping cream

freshly grated nutmeg

2 cups thinly sliced mushrooms

3–4 tablespoons dry bread crumbs

salt and freshly ground black pepper

1 Combine the wine, water, shallots and bay leaf in a medium saucepan. Bring to a boil, reduce the heat and simmer for 10 minutes. Add the scallops, cover and simmer for 3–4 minutes, until they are opaque.

2 Remove the scallops from the cooking liquid with a slotted spoon. Boil the liquid until reduced to ¾ cup. Strain into a bowl and set aside.

3 Carefully pull off the tough muscle from the side of the scallops and discard. Slice the scallops in half crosswise.

4 Melt 2 tablespoons of the butter in a heavy saucepan over medium heat. Stir in the flour and cook for 2 minutes. Add the reserved cooking liquid, whisking vigorously until smooth, then whisk in the cream and season to taste with salt, pepper and nutmeg. Reduce the heat and simmer, stirring frequently, for 10 minutes.

5 Melt the remaining butter in a skillet over medium heat. Add the mushrooms and cook, stirring frequently, for about 5 minutes, until they are lightly browned. Stir the mushrooms into the sauce.

6 Preheat the broiler. Add the scallops to the sauce and adjust the seasoning. Spoon the mixture into four individual gratin dishes, large scallop shells or a flameproof dish and sprinkle evenly with the bread crumbs. Broil until golden brown and bubbly. Serve at once.

Smoked Salmon Terrine with Lemons

Lemons can be cut and sliced in so many ways. This melt-in-the-mouth smoked salmon terrine gives a time-honored side dish an intriguing new twist.

Serves 6

4 sheets of leaf gelatin
¼ cup water
14 ounces smoked salmon, sliced
1½ cups cream cheese
½ cup crème fraîche
2 tablespoons dill mustard
juice of 1 lime

For the garnish
2 lemons
piece of cheesecloth
raffia, for tying

2 Set aside enough of the remaining smoked salmon to make a middle layer the length of the pan. Chop the rest finely by hand or in a food processor. Beat together the cream cheese, crème fraîche and dill mustard with the chopped smoked salmon until everything is well combined.

4 Tap the pan to expel any trapped air. Fold over the over-hanging salmon slices to cover the top. Cover with plastic wrap and chill for at least 4 hours.

1 Soak the gelatin in the water in a small bowl until softened. Meanwhile, line a 1-pound loaf pan with plastic wrap. Use some of the smoked salmon to line the pan, laying the slices horizontally across the base and up the sides and leaving enough overlap to fold over the top of the filling.

3 Squeeze out the gelatin and melt gently in a small saucepan with the lime juice. Add to the smoked salmon mixture and mix thoroughly. Spoon half the mixture into the lined pan. Lay the reserved smoked salmon slices on the mixture along the length of the pan, then spoon on the rest of the filling and smooth the top.

5 Make the garnish. Cut 1 lemon in half horizontally. Wrap each half in a small square of muslin. Gather the muslin at the rounded end of the lemon and tie neatly with raffia.

6 Cut a small "V" from the side of the other lemon. Repeat at ¼ inch intervals. Turn out the terrine, then slice. Garnish with muslin-wrapped lemons and lemon "leaves."

Deep-fried Whitebait

A spicy coating on these fish gives this favorite dish a crunchy bite.

Serves 6

1 cup flour

½ teaspoon curry powder

½ teaspoon ground ginger

½ teaspoon ground cayenne pepper

pinch of salt

2½ pounds fresh or frozen
   whitebait, thawed

vegetable oil, for deep-frying

lemon wedges, to garnish

1 Combine the flour, spices and
salt in a large bowl.

2 Coat the fish in the seasoned
flour and shake off any excess.

3 Heat the oil in a large heavy
saucepan until it reaches a
temperature of 375°F. Fry the
whitebait in batches for
2–3 minutes until the fish is golden
and crispy.

4 Drain well on absorbent paper
towels. Serve hot, garnished
with lemon wedges.

Crab and Ricotta Tartlets

Use the meat from a freshly cooked crab, weighing about 1 pound, if you can. Otherwise, look for frozen brown and white crab meat.

Serves 4

2 cups flour

8 tablespoons (1 stick) butter, diced

about ¼ cup ice water

1½ cups ricotta

1 tablespoon grated onion

2 tablespoons grated Parmesan cheese

½ teaspoon mustard powder

2 eggs, plus 1 egg yolk

8 ounces crab meat

2 tablespoons chopped fresh parsley

½–1 teaspoon anchovy paste

1–2 teaspoons lemon juice

salt and cayenne pepper

salad greens, to garnish

1 Sift the flour and a good pinch of salt into a mixing bowl, add the diced butter and rub it in with your fingertips, until the mixture resembles fine bread crumbs. Gradually stir in enough ice water to make a firm dough.

2 Turn the dough onto a floured surface and knead lightly. Roll out the pastry and use to line four 4-inch tartlet tins. Prick the bases with a fork, then chill in the refrigerator for 30 minutes.

3 Line the pastry shells with waxed paper and fill with baking beans. Bake in a preheated oven at 400°F for 10 minutes, then remove the paper and beans. Return to the oven and bake for another 10 minutes.

4 Place the ricotta, grated onion, Parmesan and mustard in a bowl and beat until soft. Gradually beat in the eggs and egg yolk.

5 Gently stir in the crab meat and chopped parsley, then add the anchovy paste, lemon juice, and salt and cayenne pepper, to taste.

6 Remove the tarts from the oven and reduce the temperature to 350°F. Spoon the filling into the shells and bake for 20 minutes, until set and golden brown. Serve hot with a garnish of salad greens.

Shrimp and Artichoke Salad

Artichokes are very popular in Louisiana, where this recipe comes from—and the local cooks are quite willing to use canned hearts.

INGREDIENTS

Serves 4

1 garlic clove

2 teaspoons Dijon mustard

¼ cup red wine vinegar

⅔ cup olive oil

3 tablespoons shredded fresh basil leaves
    or 2 tablespoons finely chopped
    fresh parsley

1 red onion, very finely sliced

12 ounces cooked peeled shrimp

1 can (14 ounces) artichoke hearts

½ head iceberg lettuce

salt and freshly ground black pepper

1 Coarsely chop the garlic, then crush it to a pulp with 1 teaspoon salt, using the flat of a heavy knife blade.

2 Mix the garlic and mustard to a paste, then beat in the vinegar and finally the olive oil, beating hard to make a thick, creamy dressing. Season with freshly ground black pepper and, if necessary, additional salt.

3 Stir the fresh basil into the dressing, followed by the finely sliced red onion. Let stand for 30 minutes at room temperature, then stir in the shrimp and chill in the refrigerator for 1 hour or until ready to serve.

4 Drain the artichoke hearts and halve each one. Shred the lettuce finely.

5 Make a bed of lettuce on a serving platter or 4 individual salad plates and spread the artichoke hearts over it.

6 Immediately before serving, pour the shrimp and sliced onion and their marinade on top of the salad.

Mussels Steamed in White Wine

This is the best and easiest way to serve the small, tender mussels, bouchots, which are farmed along much of the French coastline. Serve with plenty of crusty French bread to dip in the juices.

INGREDIENTS

Serves 4

4–4½ pounds mussels

1¼ cups dry white wine

4–6 large shallots, finely chopped

bouquet garni

freshly ground black pepper

1 Discard any broken mussels and those with open shells that do not close immediately when tapped sharply. Under cold running water, scrape the mussel shells with a knife to remove any barnacles and pull out the stringy "beards." Soak the mussels in several changes of cold water for at least 1 hour.

2 In a large heavy flameproof casserole, combine the white wine, shallots, bouquet garni and plenty of pepper. Bring to a boil over medium-high heat and cook for 2 minutes.

3 Add the mussels to the casserole, cover tightly and cook, shaking and tossing the pan occasionally, for 5 minutes or until the mussels have opened. Discard any mussels that have not opened.

4 Using a slotted spoon, divide the mussels among 4 warmed soup plates. Tilt the casserole a little and hold for a few seconds to let any sand sink to the bottom and settle. Alternatively, strain the cooking liquid through clean muslin into a bowl.

5 Spoon or pour the cooking liquid over the mussels and serve immediately.

VARIATION

For Mussels with Cream Sauce, cook the shellfish as described here, but transfer the mussels to a warmed bowl and cover to keep warm. Strain the cooking liquid through a muslin-lined sieve into a large saucepan and boil for about 7–10 minutes to reduce by half. Stir in 6 tablespoons whipping cream and 2 tablespoons chopped fresh parsley, then add the mussels. Cook for about 1 more minute to reheat the mussels.

PIES & BAKED DISHES

Creamy Fish and Mushroom Pie

Fish pie is a healthy and hearty dish for a hungry family. Mushrooms go well with the fish and provide additional flavor and nourishment.

Serves 4

8 ounces assorted wild and cultivated mushrooms, such as oyster, button or chanterelle, trimmed and quartered

1½ pounds cod or haddock fillet, skinned and diced

2½ cups milk, boiling

For the topping

2 pounds floury potatoes, quartered

2 tablespoons butter

⅔ cup milk

salt and freshly ground black pepper

grated nutmeg

For the sauce

4 tablespoons (½ stick) unsalted butter

1 medium onion, chopped

½ celery stalk, chopped

2 tablespoons flour

2 teaspoons lemon juice

3 tablespoons chopped fresh parsley

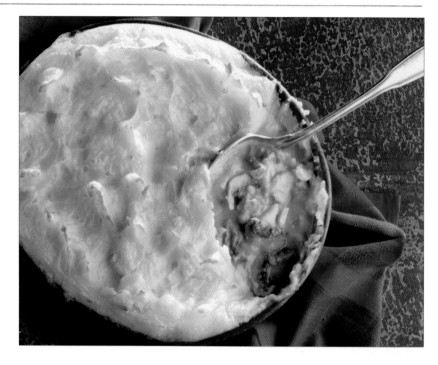

1 Grease an ovenproof dish, scatter the mushrooms over the base, add the fish and season with salt and pepper to taste. Pour in the boiling milk, cover the dish and cook at 400°F for 20 minutes.

2 Using a slotted spoon, transfer the fish and mushrooms to a 6-cup baking dish. Pour the poaching liquid into a bowl and reserve for use in the sauce.

3 Meanwhile, cook the potatoes in lightly salted boiling water for 20 minutes. Drain and mash with the butter and milk. Season well with salt, pepper and nutmeg.

4 To make the sauce, melt the butter in a saucepan, add the onion and celery and fry until soft, but not colored. Stir in the flour, then remove from the heat.

5 Gradually add the reserved liquid, stirring until absorbed. Return to the heat, stir and simmer to thicken. Add the lemon juice and parsley, season, then add to the baking dish.

6 Top with the mashed potatoes and return to the oven for 30–40 minutes, until the topping is golden brown.

Salmon Coulibiac

This is a complicated Russian dish that takes a lot of preparation, but is well worth the work. Traditionally sturgeon is used but, as this is difficult to obtain, salmon may be substituted. As a special treat, serve with shots of chilled vodka for an authentic Russian flavor.

INGREDIENTS

Serves 8

butter, for greasing

flour, for dusting

1 pound puff pastry

1 egg, beaten

salt and freshly ground black pepper

lemon wedges and fresh dill sprigs,
   to garnish

For the pancakes

2 eggs, separated

3 cups milk

1 cup flour

3 sticks butter, melted

½ teaspoon salt

½ teaspoon superfine sugar

For the filling

4 tablespoons (½ stick) butter

12 ounces chestnut mushrooms, sliced

scant ½ cup white wine

juice of ½ lemon

1½ pounds salmon fillet, skinned

1 cup long grain rice

2 tablespoons chopped fresh dill

1 large onion, chopped

4 hard-cooked eggs, shelled and sliced

1 First, make the pancakes. Whisk the egg yolks together and add the milk. Gradually beat in the flour, the melted butter (reserving 1 tablespoon), salt and sugar until smooth. Let stand for about 30 minutes.

2 Whisk the egg whites until they just form stiff peaks, then fold into the batter. Heat a little of the remaining butter in a heavy frying pan and add about 3 tablespoons of the batter. Turn and cook until golden. Repeat until all the mixture has been used up, brushing on a little melted butter when stacking the pancakes. When they are cool, cut into long rectangles, cover and set aside.

3 For the filling, melt most of the butter in a heavy frying pan, add the mushrooms and cook for 3 minutes. Add ¼ cup of the wine and boil for 2 minutes, then simmer for about 5 more minutes. Add almost all the remaining wine and the lemon juice.

4 Place the salmon on top of the cooked mushrooms, cover with foil, and gently steam for 8–10 minutes, until just cooked. Remove the salmon from the pan and set aside.

5 Set aside the mushrooms and pour the cooking liquid into a large clean pan. Add the rice and cook for 10–15 minutes, until tender, adding more wine if necessary. Remove from the heat and stir in the dill and seasoning. Melt the remaining butter and fry the onion until brown. Set aside.

6 Grease a large baking sheet. Flour a clean dish towel, place the pastry on it and roll into a 12 x 20-inch rectangle. Leaving 1¼ inches at the top and bottom ends of the pastry, place half the pancakes in a strip up the middle of the dough. Top with half the rice, half the onion, half the eggs and half the mushrooms. Place the salmon on top of the mushrooms and press down gently. Continue the layering process in reverse.

7 Take the 1¼-inch ends and wrap over the filling, then fold over the long edges. Brush with beaten egg and transfer to the baking sheet, rolling it so that it ends up seam side down. Chill for 1 hour. Cut 4 small slits in the top, brush with beaten egg and bake at 425°F for 10 minutes. Turn the oven down to 375°F and cook for another 30 minutes, until golden brown. Serve sliced, garnished with lemon and dill.

Stuffed Fish

Every community in India prepares stuffed fish, but the Parsi version must rank at the top of the list. The most popular fish in India is the pomfret. It is available at Indian grocers or large supermarkets.

INGREDIENTS

Serves 4

2 large pomfrets or Dover or lemon sole
2 teaspoons salt
juice of 1 lemon
slices of lime, to serve

For the masala

½ cup dry shredded coconut
1 small bunch fresh cilantro
8 fresh green chilies (or to taste)
1 teaspoon cumin seeds
6 garlic cloves
2 teaspoons superfine sugar
2 teaspoons lemon juice

1 Scale the fish and cut off the fins. Gut the fish and remove the heads, if desired. Using a sharp knife, make 2 diagonal slashes on each side, rinse well, then pat dry with paper towels.

2 Rub the fish inside and out with salt and lemon juice and let stand for 1 hour. Pat dry thoroughly with paper towels.

3 For the masala, grind all the ingredients together using a mortar and pestle or food processor. Stuff the fish with the masala mixture and rub any remaining masala into the gashes and all over the fish on both sides.

4 Place each fish on a separate piece of greased foil. Tightly wrap the foil over each fish. Place in a steamer and steam for 20 minutes or bake at 400°F for 30 minutes, or until cooked. Serve with slices of lime.

COOK'S TIP

In India, this fish dish is always steamed wrapped in banana leaves. Banana leaves are available at Indian or Chinese markets, but grape leaves may be used instead.

Smoked Haddock Lyonnaise

Lyonnaise dishes take their name from the city of Lyons, known for its excellent food. The term "Lyonnaise" refers to dishes prepared or garnished with onions.

INGREDIENTS

Serves 4

1 pound smoked haddock

⅔ cup milk

1 tablespoon butter

2 onions, chopped

1 tablespoon cornstarch

⅔ cup plain yogurt

1 teaspoon ground turmeric

1 teaspoon paprika

4 ounces mushrooms, sliced

2 celery stalks, chopped

2 tablespoons olive oil

12 ounces firm cooked potatoes, preferably cold, diced

1–2 ounces soft white bread crumbs

salt and freshly ground black pepper

flat leaf parsley, to garnish

2 Melt the butter and fry half the chopped onions until translucent. Stir in the cornstarch, then gradually blend in the fish cooking liquid and the yogurt and cook until thickened and smooth.

3 Stir in the turmeric, paprika, mushrooms and celery. Season to taste and add the flaked fish. Spoon into an ovenproof dish.

4 Heat the oil and fry the remaining onions until translucent. Add the diced potatoes and stir until lightly coated in oil. Sprinkle on the bread crumbs and seasoning.

5 Spoon this mixture over the fish and bake at 375°F for 20–30 minutes. Garnish with flat leaf parsley.

1 Put the smoked haddock and the milk into a large pan over low heat and poach the fish for about 15 minutes, until just cooked. Remove the haddock, reserving the cooking liquid, then flake the fish and discard the skin and any bones. Set aside.

Baked Red Snapper

The flesh of the red snapper is made tender and flavorful by rubbing in spices and baking in a sauce.

Serves 3–4

1 large red snapper, gutted and cleaned

juice of 1 lemon

½ teaspoon paprika

½ teaspoon garlic powder

½ teaspoon dried thyme

½ teaspoon freshly ground black pepper

boiled rice and lemon wedges, to serve

For the sauce

2 tablespoons vegetable oil

1 onion, chopped

1 can (14 ounces) chopped tomatoes

2 garlic cloves, crushed

1 thyme sprig or ½ teaspoon dried thyme

1 fresh green chili, seeded and
   finely chopped

½ green bell pepper, seeded and chopped

1¼ cups fish stock or water

1 Prepare the sauce. Heat the vegetable oil in a saucepan, fry the onion for 5 minutes, then add the chopped tomatoes, garlic, thyme and green chili.

2 Add the pepper and stock. Bring to a boil, stirring, then reduce the heat, cover and simmer for about 10 minutes, until the vegetables are soft. Let cool a little and then place in a blender or food processor and blend to a purée.

3 Wash the fish well and then score the skin with a sharp knife in a crisscross pattern. Combine the lemon juice, paprika, garlic, thyme and black pepper. Spoon the mixture over the fish and rub in well.

4 Place the fish in a greased baking dish and pour the sauce on top. Cover with foil and bake at 400°F for 30–40 minutes, or until the fish is cooked and flakes easily when tested with a knife. Serve with sauce from the dish, boiled rice and lemon wedges.

COOK'S TIP

If you prefer less sauce, remove the foil after 20 minutes and bake, uncovered, until cooked.

Fish Soufflé with Cheese Topping

This is an easy-going soufflé, which will not drop too much if kept waiting. On the other hand, it might be best to get the family seated before you take it out of the oven.

Serves 4

12 ounces white fish, skinned
   and boned
⅔ cup milk
4 large cooked potatoes, still warm
1 garlic clove, crushed
2 eggs, separated
grated rind and juice of ½ small lemon
4 ounces cooked peeled shrimp
2 ounces grated Cheddar cheese
salt and freshly ground black pepper

1 Place the fish in a large saucepan and add the milk. Bring just to a boil, lower the heat and cook for 12 minutes or until it flakes easily. Alternatively, place the fish and milk in a bowl and cook in the microwave for 3–4 minutes on high. Drain, reserving the milk, and place the fish in a bowl.

2 Mash the potatoes until really creamy, using as much of the reserved fish milk as necessary. Then mash in the garlic, egg yolks, lemon rind and juice and seasoning to taste.

3 Flake the fish and gently stir into the potato mixture with the shrimp. Season to taste.

4 Whisk the egg whites until stiff, but not dry, and gently fold them into the fish mixture. When smoothly blended, spoon into a greased gratin dish.

5 Sprinkle with the cheese and bake at 425°F for 25–30 minutes, until the top is golden and just about firm to the touch. (If it browns too quickly, reduce the oven temperature to 400°F.)

Roast Sea Bass

Sea bass has quite meaty flesh. It is an expensive fish, best cooked as simply as possible. Avoid elaborate sauces, which would mask its delicate flavor.

Serves 4

1 fennel bulb with fronds, about 10 ounces

2 lemons, cut in half

½ cup olive oil

1 small red onion, diced

2 sea bass, about 1¼ pounds each, cleaned with heads left on

½ cup dry white wine

salt and freshly ground black pepper

1 Preheat the oven to 375°F. Cut the fronds and green stalks off the top of the fennel and reserve. Cut the fennel bulb lengthwise into thin wedges, then into dice. Cut one half lemon into four slices. Squeeze the juice from the remaining lemon halves.

2 Heat 2 tablespoons of the oil in a skillet and sauté the fennel and onion, stirring frequently, for about 5 minutes, until softened. Remove from the heat.

3 Make three deep cuts in each side of the fish. Place in an oiled roasting tin with the fennel stalks, and tuck 2 lemon slices inside each fish. Scatter over the sautéd fennel and onion.

4 Whisk together the remaining oil, the lemon juice and seasoning, and pour over the fish. Cover with foil and roast for 30 minutes, removing the foil for the last 10 minutes. Remove the lemon slices and transfer the fish to a heated serving platter.

5 Set the roasting pan over medium heat. Add the wine and stir to incorporate all the pan juices. Bring to a boil, then spoon the juices over the fish. Garnish with the fennel fronds and lemon slices and serve.

Whole Cooked Salmon

Farmed salmon has made this fish more affordable and less of a treat, but a whole salmon still makes a great centerpiece at parties. It is never served with cold meats, but is usually accompanied by salads and mayonnaise. As with all fish, the taste depends on freshness and on not overcooking it, so although you need to start the preparation early, the cooking time is short.

INGREDIENTS

Serves about 10 as part of a buffet

1 fresh whole salmon, 5–6 pounds

2 tablespoons oil

1 lemon

salt and freshly ground black pepper

lemon wedges, cucumber and fresh dill
    sprigs, to garnish

1 Wash the salmon and dry it well, inside and out. Pour half the oil onto a large piece of strong foil and place the fish in the center.

2 Put a few slices of lemon inside the salmon and arrange some more on the top. Season well and sprinkle on the remaining oil. Wrap up the foil to make a loose parcel. Put the parcel on another sheet of foil or a baking sheet and bake at 400°F for 10 minutes. Turn off the oven, do not open the door and let sit for several hours.

3 To serve the same day, remove the foil and peel off the skin. If you are keeping it for the following day, leave the skin on and chill the fish overnight. Arrange the fish on a large platter and garnish with lemon wedges, cucumber cut into thin ribbons and sprigs of dill.

Shrimp Soufflé

This makes a very elegant lunch dish and is simple to prepare.

Serves 4–6

2 tablespoons butter, plus extra for greasing

1 tablespoon dried white bread crumbs

6 ounces cooked peeled shrimp, deveined and coarsely chopped

1 tablespoon finely chopped fresh tarragon or parsley

3 tablespoons sherry or dry white wine

freshly ground black pepper

lemon slices, whole shrimp and flat leaf parsley sprig, to garnish

For the soufflé mixture

3 tablespoons butter

2½ tablespoons flour

1 cup milk, heated

4 eggs, separated, plus 1 egg white

salt

1 Butter a 7-cup soufflé dish. Sprinkle with the bread crumbs, tilting the dish to coat the bottom and sides evenly.

2 Melt the butter in a small saucepan. Add the chopped shrimp and cook for 2–3 minutes over low heat. Stir in the tarragon or parsley and sherry and season with pepper. Cook for another 1–2 minutes. Raise the heat and boil rapidly to evaporate the liquid, then remove from the heat and set aside.

3 To make the soufflé mixture, melt the butter in a heavy saucepan. Add the flour, blending well with a wire whisk. Cook over low heat for 2–3 minutes. Pour in the hot milk and whisk vigorously until smooth. Simmer for 2 minutes, still whisking, then season to taste with salt.

4 Remove the pan from the heat and immediately beat in the egg yolks, 1 at a time. Stir in the shrimp mixture.

5 Whisk the egg whites in a large bowl until they form stiff peaks. Stir about one-quarter of the egg whites into the shrimp mixture, then gently fold in the rest of the egg whites.

6 Carefully turn the mixture into the prepared dish. Bake at 375°F for 30–40 minutes, until the soufflé is puffed up and light golden brown on top. Serve immediately, with lemon slices, whole shrimp and a parsley sprig garnish.

VARIATIONS

For lobster soufflé, substitute 1 large lobster tail for the cooked shrimp. Chop it finely and add to the saucepan with the herbs and wine in place of the shrimp. For crab soufflé, instead of shrimp, use about 6-ounces fresh crab meat or a 7-ounce can, drained. Flake and pick over carefully to remove any bits of shell.

Crab with Scallions and Ginger

This recipe is far less complicated to make than it first appears. Buy live crabs, if you can, for the best flavor and texture.

Serves 4

1 large or 2 medium crabs, cooked,
    weighing about 1½ pounds in total
2 tablespoons Chinese rice wine or
    dry sherry
1 egg, lightly beaten
1 tablespoon cornstarch paste
3–4 tablespoons vegetable oil
1 tablespoon finely chopped
    fresh ginger
3–4 scallions, cut into short sections
2 tablespoons light soy sauce
1 teaspoon light brown sugar
about 5 tablespoons vegetable or
    chicken stock
few drops sesame oil
shredded scallion, to garnish
stir-fried noodles, to serve

3 Heat the oil in a preheated wok and stir-fry the crab pieces, together with the chopped ginger and scallions, for 2–3 minutes.

4 Add the soy sauce, sugar and stock and blend well. Bring to a boil, cover and braise for 3–4 minutes. Sprinkle with sesame oil, garnish with scallions and serve with stir-fried noodles.

1 Cut the crab in half from the underbelly. Break off the claws and crack them with the back of a cleaver. Discard the legs and crack the shell, breaking it into several pieces. Discard the feathery gills and the sac.

2 Put the crab pieces in a bowl. Combine the rice wine or sherry, egg and cornstarch paste, pour over the crab and set aside to marinate for 10–15 minutes.

Seafood in Puff Pastry

This classic combination of seafood in a creamy sauce served in a puff pastry case is found as an hors d'oeuvre on the menus of many elegant restaurants in France.

Serves 6

butter, for greasing

12 ounces puff pastry

1 egg beaten with 1 tablespoon water, to glaze

¼ cup dry white wine

2 shallots, finely chopped

1 pound mussels, scrubbed and "debearded"

1 tablespoon butter

1 pound shelled scallops, cut in half horizontally

1 pound raw shrimp, peeled and deveined

6 ounces cooked lobster meat, sliced

For the sauce

2 sticks unsalted butter, diced

2 shallots, finely chopped

1 cup fish stock

6 tablespoons dry white wine

1–2 tablespoons heavy cream

lemon juice

salt and freshly ground white pepper

fresh dill sprigs, to garnish

1 Lightly grease a large baking sheet and sprinkle with a little water. On a lightly floured surface, roll out the pastry into a rectangle slightly less than ¼ inch thick. Using a sharp knife, cut into 6 diamond shapes about 5 inches long. Transfer to the baking sheet. Brush the pastry with the egg glaze. Using the tip of a knife, score a line ½ inch from the edge, then lightly mark the center in a crisscross pattern.

2 Chill the pastry shells for 30 minutes. Bake at 425°F for about 20 minutes, until puffed and golden brown. Transfer to a wire rack and, while still hot, remove each lid, cutting along the scored line to free it. Scoop out any uncooked dough from the bases and discard, then set the shells aside and let them cool completely.

3 In a large saucepan, bring the wine and shallots to a boil over high heat. Add the mussels to the pan, cover tightly and cook, shaking the pan occasionally, for 4–6 minutes, until the shells open. Remove and discard any mussels that do not open. Reserve 6 mussels for the garnish, then remove the rest of the mussels from their shells and set aside in a bowl, covered. Strain the cooking liquid through a muslin-lined sieve and reserve for the sauce.

4 In a heavy frying pan, melt the butter over medium heat. Add the scallops and shrimp, cover tightly and cook for 3–4 minutes, shaking and stirring occasionally, until they feel just firm to the touch; do not overcook.

5 Using a slotted spoon, transfer the scallops and shrimp to the bowl with the mussels and add any cooking juices to the reserved mussel cooking liquid.

6 To make the sauce, melt 2 tablespoons of the butter in a heavy saucepan. Add the shallots and cook for 2 minutes. Pour in the fish stock and boil for about 15 minutes over high heat, until reduced by three-quarters. Add the white wine and reserved cooking liquid and boil for 5–7 minutes, until reduced by half. Lower the heat to medium and whisk in the remaining butter, a little at a time, to make a smooth thick sauce (lift the pan from the heat if the sauce begins to boil). Whisk in the cream and season with salt, if needed, pepper and lemon juice. Keep the sauce warm over very low heat, stirring frequently.

7 Warm the pastry shells in a low oven for about 10 minutes. Put the mussels, scallops and shrimp in a large saucepan. Stir in a quarter of the sauce and reheat gently over low heat. Gently stir in the lobster meat and cook for 1 more minute.

8 Arrange the pastry shell bases on individual plates. Divide the seafood mixture equally among them and top with the lids. Garnish each with a mussel in its half shell and a dill sprig and spoon the remaining sauce around the edges or serve separately.

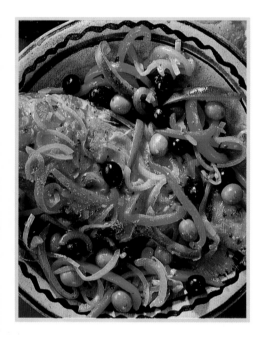

FRIED &
BROILED DISHES

Pan-fried Sole with Lemon

The delicate flavor and texture of sole can be enjoyed to the full in this simple, classic recipe. Lemon sole is used here because it is easier to obtain and less expensive than Dover sole.

INGREDIENTS

Serves 2

2–3 tablespoons all-purpose flour

4 lemon sole fillets

3 tablespoons olive oil

¼ cup butter

4 tablespoons lemon juice

2 tablespoons bottled capers, drained and rinsed

salt and freshly ground black pepper

fresh flat leaf parsley and lemon wedges, to garnish

1 Season the flour with salt and black pepper. Coat the lemon sole fillets with the seasoned flour evenly on both sides, shaking off any excess. Heat the olive oil with half the butter in a large shallow saucepan or skillet until foaming. Add two of the lemon sole fillets and fry over medium heat for about 2–3 minutes on each side, until golden.

2 Carefully lift out the sole fillets with a fish slice and place them on a warm serving platter. Cover with foil and keep hot. Fry the remaining sole fillets in the same way and transfer them to the serving platter.

3 Remove the pan from the heat and stir in the lemon juice and the remaining butter. Return the pan to high heat and stir vigorously until the butter is fully incorporated and the pan juices are sizzling and beginning to turn golden brown. Remove from the heat and stir in the capers.

4 Pour the pan juices over the sole, sprinkle with salt and pepper to taste and garnish with the parsley. Add the lemon wedges and serve at once.

COOK'S TIP

It is important to cook the pan juices to the right color after removing the fish. Too pale, and they will taste insipid; too dark, and they may taste bitter. Take great care not to be distracted at this point so that you can watch the color of the juices change to a golden brown.

Herrings in Oatmeal with Mustard

Oatmeal makes a delicious, crunchy coating for tender herrings.

INGREDIENTS

Serves 4

1 tablespoon Dijon mustard

1½ teaspoons tarragon vinegar

¾ cup thick mayonnaise

4 herrings, about 8 ounces each, gutted
    and cleaned

1 lemon, halved

1½ cups oatmeal

salt and freshly ground black pepper

1 Beat mustard and vinegar to taste into the mayonnaise. Chill lightly.

2 Place one fish at a time on a board, cut side down and opened out. Press gently along the backbone with your thumbs. Turn over the fish and carefully lift away the backbone.

3 Squeeze lemon juice over both sides of the fish, then season with salt and pepper. Fold the fish in half, skin side outward.

4 Place the oatmeal on a plate, then coat each herring evenly in the oatmeal, pressing it in gently but firmly.

5 Place the herrings on a broiler pan and broil for 3–4 minutes on each side, until the skin is golden brown and crisp and the flesh flakes easily. Serve immediately with the mustard sauce, served separately.

Fish and Chips

This classic British dish is quick and easy to make at home.

INGREDIENTS

Serves 4

1 cup self-rising flour

⅔ cup water

1½ pounds potatoes

oil, for deep-frying

1½-pound piece skinned cod fillet, cut
    into 4 pieces

salt

lemon wedges, to garnish

1 Sift the flour and a pinch of salt together in a bowl, then form a well in the center. Gradually pour in the water, whisking in the flour to make a smooth batter. Set aside to rest for 30 minutes.

2 Cut the potatoes into strips about ½ inch wide and 2 inches long. Place them in a colander and rinse in cold water, then drain and dry well.

3 Heat the oil in a deep-fat fryer or large heavy pan to 300°F. Using the wire basket, lower the potatoes in batches into the oil and cook for 5–6 minutes, shaking the basket occasionally, until the potatoes are soft but not browned. Remove the chips from the oil and drain thoroughly on paper towels.

4 Heat the oil in the fryer to 375°F. Season the fish. Stir the batter, then dip the pieces of fish into it, in turn, letting the excess drain off.

5 Working in two batches if necessary, lower the fish into the oil and fry for 6–8 minutes, until crisp and golden brown. Drain the fish on paper towels and keep warm.

6 Add the chips in batches to the oil and cook for 2–3 minutes, until golden brown and crisp. Keep hot. Sprinkle with salt and serve with the fish, garnished with lemon wedges.

Fish Steaks with Cilantro-lime Butter

Citrus-flavored butter adds just the right kind of zip to fish steaks.

INGREDIENTS

Serves 4

1½ pounds swordfish or tuna steak,
 1 inch thick, cut into 4 pieces
¼ cup vegetable oil
2 tablespoons lemon juice
1 tablespoon lime juice
salt and freshly ground black pepper
cilantro-lime butter (see Cook's Tip)
asparagus and lime slices, to serve

1 Put the fish steaks in a shallow dish. Combine the oil, lemon juice and lime juice, season and pour over the fish. Cover and refrigerate for 1–2 hours, turning the fish once or twice.

2 Drain the fish steaks and arrange on a hot broiler pan, or set over the hot charcoal about 5 inches from the coals. Grill for 3–4 minutes or until the fish is just firm to the touch but still moist in the center, turning the steaks over once.

3 Transfer to warmed plates and top each fish steak with a pat of cilantro-lime butter. Serve the fish immediately with asparagus and slices of lime.

COOK'S TIP

For cilantro-lime butter, finely chop 1 small bunch fresh cilantro. Mix into 1 stick softened, unsalted butter, together with the grated rind and juice of 1 lime. Roll the butter neatly in waxed paper and chill in the refrigerator until firm. Other flavored butters can be made in the same way. Try parsley-lemon butter, made from 2 tablespoons chopped parsley, 1 stick unsalted butter and 1 tablespoon lemon juice.

Turkish Cold Fish

Cold fish dishes are appreciated in the Middle East and for good reason—they are delicious. This particular version from Turkey can be made using mackerel, if preferred.

INGREDIENTS

Serves 4

¼ cup olive oil

2 pounds porgy or snapper

2 onions, sliced

1 green bell pepper, seeded and sliced

1 red bell pepper, seeded and sliced

3 garlic cloves, crushed

1 tablespoon tomato paste

¼ cup fish stock, bottled clam juice or
    water

5–6 tomatoes, skinned and sliced or 1 can
    (14 ounces) tomatoes

2 tablespoons chopped fresh parsley

2 tablespoons lemon juice

1 teaspoon paprika

15–20 green and black olives

salt and freshly ground black pepper

bread and salad, to serve

1 Heat 2 tablespoons of the oil in a large roasting pan or frying pan and fry the fish on both sides until golden brown. Remove from the pan, cover and keep warm.

2 Heat the remaining oil in the pan and fry the onion for 2–3 minutes, until softened. Add the peppers and continue cooking for 3–4 minutes, stirring occasionally, then add the garlic and stir-fry for 1 more minute.

3 Blend the tomato paste with the fish stock, clam juice or water and stir into the pan with the tomatoes, parsley, lemon juice, paprika and seasoning. Simmer very gently for 15 minutes, stirring occasionally.

4 Return the fish to the pan and cover with the sauce. Cook for 10 minutes, then add the olives and cook for another 5 minutes or until just cooked through.

5 Transfer the fish to a serving dish and pour the sauce on top. Let cool, then cover and chill until completely cold. Serve cold with bread and salad.

COOK'S TIP

One large fish looks spectacular, but it is tricky both to cook and to serve. If you prefer, buy 4 smaller fish and cook for a shorter time, until just tender and cooked through.

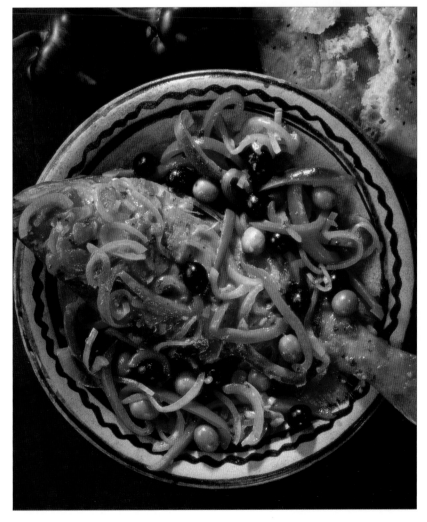

Salmon Cakes with Spicy Mayonnaise

Taste the difference between home-made fish cakes and the inferior store-bought variety with this delicious recipe.

INGREDIENTS

Serves 4

2 boiling potatoes, about 12 ounces

12 ounces salmon fillet, skinned and
    finely chopped

2–3 tablespoons chopped fresh dill

1 tablespoon lemon juice

flour, for coating

3 tablespoons vegetable oil

salt and freshly ground black pepper

spicy mayonnaise (see Cook's Tip) and
    salad greens, to serve

1 Put the potatoes in a saucepan of boiling salted water and parboil them for 15 minutes.

2 Meanwhile, combine the salmon, dill, lemon juice, salt and pepper in a large bowl.

3 Drain the potatoes and let them cool. When they are cool enough to handle, peel away the skins.

4 Shred the potatoes into strips on the coarse side of a grater.

5 Add to the salmon mixture. Combine gently with your fingers, breaking up the strips of potato as little as possible.

6 Divide the salmon and potato mixture into 8 portions. Shape each into a compact cake, pressing well together. Flatten the cakes to about ½ inch thickness.

7 Coat the salmon cakes lightly with flour, shaking off excess.

8 Heat the oil in a large frying pan. Add the salmon cakes and fry for 5 minutes or until crisp and golden brown on both sides.

9 Drain the salmon cakes on paper towels and serve with the spicy mayonnaise and salad.

COOK'S TIP
~

To make spicy mayonnaise, combine 1½ cups mayonnaise, 2 teaspoons Dijon mustard, ½–1 teaspoon Worcestershire sauce and a dash of Tabasco sauce. You can use home-made or good quality commercial mayonnaise.

Whiting Fillets in a Polenta Crust

Polenta is sometimes called cornmeal. Use instant polenta if you can, as it will give a better crunchy coating.

Serves 4

8 small whiting fillets

finely grated rind of 1 lemon

8 ounces polenta

2 tablespoons olive oil

1 tablespoon butter

2 tablespoons mixed fresh herbs, such as
   parsley, chervil and chives

salt and freshly ground black pepper

toasted pine nuts and red onion, sliced,
   to garnish

steamed spinach, to serve

1 Make 4 small cuts in each fillet to prevent the fish from curling up when it is cooked.

2 Sprinkle the seasoning and lemon rind over the fish.

3 Press the polenta onto the fillets. Chill in the refrigerator for 30 minutes.

4 Heat the oil and butter in a large frying pan and gently fry the fillets on each side for 3–4 minutes. Sprinkle on the fresh herbs and garnish with toasted pine nuts and red onion slices. Serve with steamed spinach.

Monkfish with Peppered Citrus Marinade

Monkfish is a firm, meaty fish that cooks well on the barbecue and keeps its shape.

INGREDIENTS

Serves 4

2 monkfish tails, about 12 ounces each
1 lime
1 lemon
2 oranges
handful of fresh thyme sprigs
2 tablespoons olive oil
1 tablespoon mixed peppercorns, roughly crushed
salt and freshly ground black pepper
lemon and lime wedges, to serve

1 Remove any skin from the monkfish tails. Cut carefully down one side of the backbone, sliding the knife between the bone and flesh, to remove the fillet on one side. You can ask your fishmonger to do this for you.

2 Turn the fish and repeat on the other side, to remove the second fillet. Repeat on the second tail. Lay the 4 fillets out flat.

3 Cut 2 slices each from the lime, lemon and 1 orange and arrange them over 2 of the fillets. Add a few sprigs of thyme and sprinkle with salt and pepper. Finely grate the rind from the remaining fruit and sprinkle it over the fish.

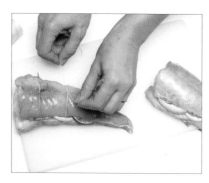

4 Lay the remaining 2 fish fillets on top and tie them firmly with fine cotton string to hold them in shape. Arrange them in a wide dish.

5 Squeeze the juice from the remaining lime, lemon and oranges and mix it with the oil and more salt and pepper to taste. Spoon over the fish. Cover and let marinate for about 1 hour, turning occasionally and spooning the marinade over it.

6 Drain the monkfish, reserving the marinade, and sprinkle with the crushed peppercorns. Cook on a medium-hot barbecue for 15–20 minutes, basting it with the marinade and turning it occasionally, until it is evenly cooked through. Serve with lemon and lime wedges.

VARIATION

You can also use this marinade for monkfish kebabs.

Fish Fillets with Orange and Tomato Sauce

Citrus flavors liven up any plain white fish beautifully.

INGREDIENTS

Serves 4

3 tablespoons flour

4 fillets of firm white fish, such as cod, sea bass or sole, about 1½ pounds

1 tablespoon butter or margarine

2 tablespoons olive oil

1 onion, sliced

2 garlic cloves, chopped

¼ teaspoon ground cumin

1¼ pounds tomatoes, skinned, seeded and chopped, or 1 can (14 ounces) chopped tomatoes

½ cup fresh orange juice

salt and freshly ground black pepper

orange wedges, for garnishing

1 Put the flour on a plate and season well with salt and pepper. Coat the fish fillets lightly with the seasoned flour, shaking off any excess.

2 Heat the butter and half the oil in a large frying pan. Add the fish fillets to the pan and cook for about 3 minutes on each side, until golden brown and the flesh flakes easily when tested with a fork.

3 When the fish is cooked, transfer to a warmed serving platter. Cover with foil and keep warm while you make the sauce.

4 Heat the remaining oil in the pan. Add the onion and garlic and cook for about 5 minutes, until softened but not colored.

5 Stir in the ground cumin, tomatoes and orange juice. Bring to a boil and cook, stirring frequently, for about 10 minutes, until thickened.

6 Garnish the fish with orange wedges and serve immediately, passing the sauce separately.

Cajun-style Cod

This recipe works equally well with any firm-fleshed fish, such as swordfish, shark, tuna or halibut.

Serves 4

4 cod steaks, each weighing about
  6 ounces

2 tablespoons plain yogurt

1 tablespoon lime or lemon juice

1 garlic clove, crushed

1 teaspoon ground cumin

1 teaspoon paprika

1 teaspoon mustard powder

½ teaspoon cayenne powder

½ teaspoon dried thyme

½ teaspoon oregano

vegetable oil, for brushing

new potatoes and mixed greens,
  to serve

1 Pat the fish dry on absorbent paper towels. Combine the yogurt and lime juice and brush lightly over both sides of the fish.

2 Combine the garlic, cumin, paprika, mustard powder, cayenne, thyme and oregano. Coat both sides of the fish with the seasoning mix, rubbing in well.

3 Brush a ridged grill pan or heavy frying pan with a little oil. Heat until very hot. Add the fish and cook over high heat for 4 minutes or until the underside is well browned.

4 Brush the fish with a little more oil, if necessary, turn over and cook for another 4 minutes or until the steaks have cooked through. Serve immediately, accompanied with new potatoes and mixed greens.

Marinated Fish

This dish is of Spanish origin and is also very popular throughout the Caribbean.

Serves 4–6

1½ teaspoons garlic powder

½ teaspoon coarse-grain black pepper

½ teaspoon paprika

½ teaspoon celery salt

½ teaspoon curry powder

2 pounds cod fillet

½ lemon

1 tablespoon seasoned salt

flour, for dusting

oil, for frying

lemon wedges, to garnish

For the sauce

2 tablespoons vegetable oil

1 onion, sliced

½ red bell pepper, sliced

½ christophene or chayote, peeled and
    seeded, cut into small pieces

2 garlic cloves, crushed

½ cup malt vinegar

5 tablespoons water

½ teaspoon ground allspice

1 bay leaf

1 small hot pepper, chopped

1 tablespoon dark brown sugar

salt and freshly ground black pepper

1 Combine all the spices. Place the fish in a shallow dish, squeeze on the lemon, then sprinkle with the seasoned salt and pat into the fish. Let marinate in a cool place for 1 hour.

2 Cut the fish into 3-inch pieces and dust with a little flour, shaking off the excess.

3 Heat the oil in a heavy frying pan and fry the fish pieces for 2–3 minutes, until golden brown and crisp, turning occasionally.

4 To make the sauce, heat the oil in a heavy frying pan and fry the onion until soft. Add the pepper, christophene or chayote and garlic and stir-fry for 2 minutes. Pour in the vinegar, add the remaining ingredients and simmer gently for 5 minutes. Let stand for 10 minutes, then pour the sauce over the fish. Serve hot, garnished with lemon wedges.

Lobster Thermidor

Lobster Thermidor takes its name from the eleventh month of the French Revolutionary calendar, which falls in midsummer, although this rich dish is equally delicious in colder weather, too. Serve one lobster per person as a main course or one filled shell each for an appetizer.

INGREDIENTS

Serves 2–4

2 live lobsters, about 1½ pounds each

1½ tablespoons butter

2 tablespoons all-purpose flour

2 tablespoons brandy

½ cup milk

6 tablespoons whipping cream

1 tablespoon Dijon mustard

lemon juice

salt and freshly ground white pepper

grated Parmesan cheese,
    for sprinkling

fresh parsley and dill, to garnish

1 Bring a large saucepan of lightly salted water to a boil. Plunge the lobsters into the pan head first and cook for between 8–10 minutes.

2 Remove the lobsters from the pan and cut them in half lengthwise. Discard the dark sac behind the eyes, then pull out the string-like intestine from the tail. Remove the meat from the shells, reserving the coral and liver, then rinse the shells and wipe dry. Cut the meat into bite-size pieces.

3 Melt the butter in a heavy-based saucepan over medium heat. Add the flour and cook, stirring constantly, until it is just turning golden. Pour in the brandy and milk, whisking vigorously until smooth, then whisk in the cream and mustard.

4 Press the lobster coral and liver through a strainer into the sauce and whisk to blend. Reduce the heat to low and simmer gently, stirring frequently, for about 10 minutes, until thickened. Season with salt, if necessary, pepper and lemon juice.

5 Preheat the broiler. Arrange the lobster shells in a gratin dish or shallow flameproof dish.

6 Stir the lobster meat into the sauce and divide the mixture between the shells. Sprinkle with Parmesan and broil until golden. Serve garnished with herbs.

Cauliflower, Shrimp and Broccoli Tempura

All sorts of vegetables are delicious deep fried in this Japanese style. Firm vegetables, such as cauliflower and broccoli, are best blanched before frying but snow peas, slices of red and green bell pepper and mushrooms can simply be dipped in the batter and fried.

INGREDIENTS

Serves 4

½ cauliflower

10 ounces broccoli

8 raw shrimp

8 button mushrooms (optional)

sunflower or vegetable oil,
   for deep-frying

lemon wedges and sprigs of cilantro,
   to garnish (optional)

soy sauce, to serve

For the batter

1 cup all-purpose flour

pinch of salt

2 eggs, separated

¾ cup ice water

2 tablespoons sunflower or vegetable oil

1 Cut the cauliflower and broccoli into medium-size flowerets. Blanch all the flowerets for 1–2 minutes. Drain, rinse under cold running water and set aside. Peel the shrimp, but leave their tails intact, and set aside.

COOK'S TIP

Try cooking other vegetables in this way, such as eggplants and zucchini, or even celery leaves.

2 To make the batter, place the flour and salt in a bowl. Blend together the egg yolk and water and stir into the flour, beating well to make a smooth batter.

3 Beat in the oil. Whisk the egg whites until stiff and then fold them into the batter. Heat the oil for deep-frying to 375°F. Coat a few of the vegetables and shrimp in the batter.

4 Fry for about 2–3 minutes, until lightly golden and puffy. Transfer to a plate lined with paper towels and keep warm while you are frying the remaining shrimp and vegetables.

5 Arrange the tempura on individual serving plates, garnish with wedges of lemon and cilantro sprigs, if desired, and serve with little bowls of soy sauce.

Jumbo Shrimp with Vermouth

The delicate herb flavoring in French vermouth perfectly offsets this delightful Mediterranean-style shrimp dish.

INGREDIENTS

Serves 4

20 raw jumbo shrimp,
   heads removed
½ cucumber
2 tablespoons butter
1 tablespoon olive oil
1 small shallot, finely chopped
¼ cup drained sun-dried tomatoes in
   oil, chopped
4 tablespoons vegetable stock
2 tablespoons vermouth
⅔ cup heavy cream
1 tablespoon chopped fennel leaves
3 tablespoons golden salmon roe
salt and freshly ground white pepper
fennel leaves, to garnish

1 Peel the shrimp, leaving the tails intact. Cut each shrimp down the back and remove the black vein. Rinse, then dry with paper towels.

2 Peel the cucumber, cut it in half lengthwise, and then scoop out the seeds. Slice the cucumber thickly into crescents.

3 Heat the butter and oil together in a large skillet, add the chopped shallot and fry over medium heat, stirring frequently, until softened.

4 Add the tomatoes, stock, vermouth and shrimp. Cook over low heat for 8–10 minutes.

5 Cook the cucumber crescents in a small pan of boiling salted water for 3 minutes, then drain.

6 Stir the cream and chopped fennel leaves into the shrimp mixture and cook until the sauce thickens. Season to taste and stir in the cooked cucumber and the salmon roe. Reheat and serve, garnished with fennel leaves.

COOK'S TIP

Try using sun-dried bell peppers instead of the tomatoes. The salmon roe adds a delicious flavor, but it is not essential.

CASSEROLES
& STEWS

Green Fish Curry

This dish combines all the typical flavors of the East.

Serves 4

¼ teaspoon ground turmeric

2 tablespoons lime juice

4 cod fillets, skinned and cut into
    2-inch chunks

1 onion, chopped

1 fresh large green chili, roughly
    chopped

1 garlic clove, crushed

½ cup cashews

½ teaspoon fennel seeds

2 tablespoons dry shredded coconut

2 tablespoons oil

¼ teaspoon cumin seeds

¼ teaspoon ground coriander

¼ teaspoon ground cumin

⅔ cup water

¾ cup light cream or half-and-half

3 tablespoons finely chopped
    fresh cilantro

salt

fresh cilantro sprig, to garnish

vegetable pilaf, to serve (optional)

1 Combine the turmeric, lime juice and a pinch of salt and rub over the fish. Cover and let marinate for 15 minutes.

2 Meanwhile work the onion, chili, garlic, cashews, fennel seeds and coconut to a paste in a food processor or in a mortar with a pestle. Spoon the paste into a bowl and set aside.

3 Heat the oil in a large frying pan and fry the cumin seeds for 2 minutes, until they begin to splutter. Add the spice paste and fry for 5 minutes, then stir in the ground coriander, cumin and water. Fry, stirring frequently, for about 2–3 minutes.

4 Add the cream or half-and-half and the fresh cilantro. Simmer for5 minutes. Add the fish and gently stir in. Cover and cook gently for 10 minutes, until the fish is tender. Garnish with a cilantro sprig and serve with vegetable pilaf, if desired.

Creole Fish Stew

A simple, attractive dish—good for an informal dinner party.

INGREDIENTS

Serves 4–6

2 whole red bream or large snapper, cleaned and cut into 1-inch pieces
2 tablespoons seasoning salt
2 tablespoons malt vinegar
flour, for dusting
oil, for frying

For the sauce

2 tablespoons vegetable oil
1 tablespoon butter or margarine
1 onion, finely chopped
2 large fresh tomatoes, skinned and finely chopped
2 garlic cloves, crushed
2 thyme sprigs
2½ cups fish stock or water
½ teaspoon ground cinnamon
1 hot chili, chopped
1 red bell pepper, finely chopped
1 green bell pepper, finely chopped
salt
oregano sprigs, to garnish

1 Sprinkle the fish with the seasoning salt and malt vinegar, turning to coat. Set aside in the refrigerator to marinate for a minimum of 2 hours, or overnight.

2 When ready to cook, place a little flour on a large plate and coat the fish pieces, shaking off any excess flour.

3 Heat a little oil in a large frying pan and fry the fish pieces for about 5 minutes, until golden brown, then set aside. Do not worry if the fish is not cooked through; it will finish cooking in the sauce.

4 To make the sauce, heat the oil and butter in a large frying pan or wok and stir-fry the onion for 5 minutes. Add the tomatoes, garlic and thyme, stir well and simmer for another 5 minutes. Stir in the stock or water, cinnamon and hot chili.

5 Add the fish pieces and the chopped red and green bell peppers. Simmer until the fish is cooked through and the stock has reduced to a thick sauce. Adjust the seasoning with salt. Serve hot, garnished with oregano.

Italian Fish Stew

Italians are renowned for enjoying good food, especially if it is shared with all the members of an extended family. This stew is a veritable feast of fish and seafood in a delicious tomato broth, suitable for a more modest family lunch.

INGREDIENTS

Serves 4

2 tablespoons olive oil

1 onion, thinly sliced

a few saffron threads

1 teaspoon dried thyme

large pinch of cayenne pepper

2 garlic cloves, finely chopped

2 cans (14 ounces each) peeled tomatoes, drained and chopped

¾ cup dry white wine

8 cups hot fish stock

12 ounces skinless white fish fillets, cut into pieces

1 pound monkfish, membrane removed, cut into pieces

1 pound mussels in the shell, scrubbed and "beards" removed

8 ounces small squid, cleaned and cut into rings

2 tablespoons chopped fresh basil or parsley

salt and freshly ground black pepper

thickly sliced bread, to serve

1 Heat the oil in a large heavy saucepan. Add the onion, saffron, thyme, cayenne pepper and salt, to taste. Stir well and cook over low heat for 8–10 minutes, until the onion is soft. Add the garlic and cook for another minute.

2 Stir in the tomatoes, wine and fish stock. Bring to a boil and boil for 1 minute, then reduce the heat and simmer gently for 15 minutes.

3 Add the white fish fillet and monkfish pieces to the pan and simmer gently over low heat for another 3 minutes.

4 Add the mussels and squid rings and simmer for about 2 minutes, until the mussels open. Discard any that remain closed. Stir in the basil or parsley and season to taste. Ladle into warmed soup bowls and serve with bread.

French Fish Stew

A traditional recipe using freshwater fish cooked in red wine and brandy; an ideal dish for entertaining.

INGREDIENTS

Serves 6

3–3½ pounds freshwater fish, such as carp, trout and skinned eel

3 tablespoons all-purpose flour

4 tablespoons butter

8 ounces smoked bacon, cut into small strips

4 shallots, very finely chopped

8 ounces small onions

3 cups mushrooms, chopped

½ cup brandy

4 cups red wine

1¼ cups veal or chicken stock

1 garlic clove, crushed

1 bouquet garni

salt and freshly ground black pepper

chopped fresh parsley, to garnish

garlic bread, to serve

1 Clean the carp and trout, remove the heads and fins, fillet the flesh and cut into slices. Cut the eel into chunks.

2 Put half of the flour into a plastic bag, season with salt and pepper, add the fish pieces and shake to coat.

3 In a large pan, melt the butter over medium heat. Add the fish pieces and brown them on both sides. Remove the fish from the pan and set aside.

4 Add the bacon, shallots and onions to the pan and cook over low heat for about 10 minutes, until golden. Stir in the chopped mushrooms and cook for a further 5 minutes.

5 Stir in the brandy and, if you wish to flambé, ignite carefully with a match, shaking the pan until the flames have died down. Add the wine, bring to a boil and simmer for 2–3 minutes.

6 Stir in the veal or chicken stock, garlic and bouquet garni. Bring to a boil and simmer over low heat for 5 minutes. Add the fish and simmer until cooked.

7 With a slotted spoon, remove the fish and keep hot. In a small bowl, blend the remaining flour with a little cold water and stir into the pan. Bring to a boil and cook for 5 minutes, then return the fish to the pan. Serve garnished with chopped parsley and accompanied by garlic bread.

COOK'S TIP

If carp is not available, use extra trout, or substitute another fish, such as monkfish, haddock or bream.

Fish Stew with Calvados, Parsley and Dill

This rustic stew harbors all sorts of interesting flavors and will please and intrigue. Many varieties of fish can be used, just choose the freshest and best.

INGREDIENTS

Serves 4

2¼ pounds assorted white fish

1 tablespoon chopped fresh parsley, few leaves to garnish

8 ounces mushrooms

1 can (8 ounces) tomatoes

1 large bunch fresh dill sprigs

2 teaspoons flour

1 tablespoon butter

2 cups cider

3 tablespoons Calvados

salt and freshly ground black pepper

1 Chop the fish roughly and place it in a casserole or stewing pot with the parsley, mushrooms, tomatoes and salt and pepper to taste. Reserve 4 dill sprigs to garnish and chop the remainder. Add the chopped dill to the casserole.

2 Work the flour into the butter with a fork. Heat the cider and stir into the flour and butter mixture with a spoon, a little at a time. Cook, stirring, until it has thickened slightly.

3 Add the cider mixture and the Calvados to the fish and mix gently. Cover and bake at 350°F for about 30 minutes or until cooked through. Serve immediately, garnished with reserved sprigs of dill and the parsley leaves.

Indian Fish Stew

A spicy fish stew made with potatoes, peppers and traditional Indian spices.

Serves 4

2 tablespoons oil

1 teaspoon cumin seeds

1 onion, chopped

1 red bell pepper, thinly sliced

1 garlic clove, crushed

2 red chilies, finely chopped

2 bay leaves

½ teaspoon salt

1 teaspoon ground cumin

1 teaspoon ground coriander

1 teaspoon chili powder

1 can (14 ounces) chopped tomatoes

2 large potatoes, cut into 1-inch chunks

1¼ cups fish stock

4 cod fillets

chappatis, to serve

1 Heat the oil in a large deep-sided frying pan and fry the cumin seeds for 2 minutes, until they begin to splutter. Add the onion, pepper, garlic, chilies and bay leaves and fry for 5–7 minutes, until the onions have browned.

2 Add the salt, ground cumin, ground coriander and chili powder and cook for 3–4 minutes.

3 Stir in the chopped tomatoes, potatoes and fish stock. Bring to a boil and simmer for another 10 minutes.

4 Add the fish, then cover and simmer for 10 minutes or until the fish is tender. Serve with freshly cooked chappatis.

Shellfish with Seasoned Broth

The robust flavor of the shellfish is perfectly offset by a delicate broth infused with fragrant vegetables.

Serves 4

1½ pounds mussels, scrubbed in cold
   water and debearded
1 small fennel bulb, thinly sliced
1 onion, thinly sliced
1 leek, thinly sliced
1 small carrot, cut in julienne strips
1 garlic clove
4 cups water
pinch of curry powder
pinch of saffron
1 bay leaf
1 pound raw jumbo shrimp, peeled
   (reserve a few in their shells,
    to garnish)
1 pound small shelled scallops
6 ounces cooked lobster meat,
   sliced (optional)
salt and freshly ground black pepper

1 Put the mussels in a large heavy-based saucepan or flameproof casserole. Cover tightly and cook over high heat, shaking the pan or casserole occasionally, for 4–6 minutes, until the shells open. When they are cool enough to handle, discard any mussels that have not opened and remove the remainder from their shells. Reserve a few in their shells to garnish, if desired. Strain the cooking liquid through a cheesecloth-lined strainer and set aside.

2 Put the fennel, onion, leek, carrot and garlic in a large saucepan and add the water, reserved mussel cooking liquid, curry powder, saffron and bay leaf. Bring to a boil and skim off any foam that rises to the surface. Then reduce the heat, cover and simmer gently for 20 minutes, until the vegetables are tender. Remove and discard the garlic clove.

3 Add the shrimp, scallops and lobster meat, if using, and simmer for 1 minute. Add the mussels and simmer over low heat for about 3 minutes, until the scallops have turned opaque and all the shellfish is heated through. Taste and adjust the seasoning, if necessary, then ladle the shellfish and broth into a warm tureen or four shallow soup plates. Garnish with the reserved mussels and prawns, and serve at once.

Crab and Corn Gumbo

Gumbos are traditional Creole dishes, which come from New Orleans, Louisiana, and always contain a roux that gives this dish a distinctly rich flavor.

INGREDIENTS

Serves 4

2 tablespoons butter or margarine

2 tablespoons flour

1 tablespoon vegetable oil

1 onion, finely chopped

4 ounces okra, trimmed and chopped

2 garlic cloves, crushed

1 tablespoon finely chopped celery

2½ cups fish stock

⅔ cup sherry

1 tablespoon ketchup

½ teaspoon dried oregano

¼ teaspoon pumpkin pie spice

2 teaspoons Worcestershire sauce

2 corn cobs, sliced

1 pound crab claws

cayenne pepper

fresh cilantro sprigs, to garnish

1 Melt the butter or margarine in a large saucepan over a low heat, add the flour and stir together to make a roux. Cook for about 10 minutes, stirring constantly to prevent burning, while the roux turns golden brown and then darkens to a rich, nutty brown. If black specks appear, the roux must be discarded. Turn the roux onto a plate and set aside.

2 Heat the oil in the same saucepan over medium heat, add the onion, okra, garlic and celery and stir to combine. Cook for a few minutes, then add the fish stock, sherry, ketchup, oregano, pumpkin pie spice, Worcestershire sauce and cayenne pepper to taste.

3 Bring to a boil, then simmer gently for about 10 minutes, until the vegetables are tender. Add the roux, stirring it well into the sauce, and cook for a few minutes, until thickened.

4 Add the corn cobs and crab claws and continue to simmer gently over low heat for about 10 minutes, until the crab and corn are cooked.

5 Spoon onto warmed serving plates and garnish with sprigs of fresh cilantro.

Ragoût of Shellfish with Sweet Scented Basil

Green curry paste is an integral part of Thai cooking and can be used to accompany other dishes made with fish or chicken. Curry pastes will keep for up to 3 weeks stored in an airtight container in the refrigerator.

INGREDIENTS

Serves 4–6

1 pound fresh mussels in their shells, scrubbed and with "beards" removed

¼ cup water

8 ounces medium squid

1⅔ cups canned coconut milk

1¼ cups chicken or vegetable stock

12 ounces monkfish, hoki or red snapper, skinned

5 ounces raw or cooked shrimp, peeled and deveined

4 scallops, sliced (optional)

4 ounces green beans, trimmed and cooked

¼ cup canned bamboo shoots, drained

1 ripe tomato, skinned, seeded, and roughly chopped

4 sprigs large-leaf basil, torn, and strips of fresh red chili, to garnish

rice, to serve (optional)

For the green curry paste

2 teaspoons coriander seeds

½ teaspoon caraway or cumin seeds

3–4 fresh green chilies, finely chopped

4 teaspoons superfine sugar

3-inch piece lemon grass

¾-in piece ginger, finely chopped

3 garlic cloves, crushed

4 shallots or 1 medium onion, finely chopped

¾-inch-square piece shrimp paste

1 cup cilantro leaves, finely chopped

3 tablespoons fresh mint or basil, finely chopped

½ teaspoon ground nutmeg

2 tablespoons vegetable oil

salt

1 Place the mussels in a large saucepan, add the water, cover and cook for 6–8 minutes, until the shells open. Take three-quarters of the mussels out of their shells and set aside. (Discard any that have not opened.) Strain the cooking liquid and set aside.

2 To prepare the squid, trim off the tentacles beneath the eye. Rinse under cold running water, discarding the gut. Remove the "quill" from inside the body and rub off the paper-thin skin. Cut the body open and score with a sharp knife. Cut into strips and set aside.

3 To make the green curry paste, dry-fry the coriander and caraway seeds in a wok to release their flavor. Grind the chilies with the sugar and 2 teaspoons salt in a mortar with a pestle or in a food processor to make a smooth paste. Combine the seeds from the wok with the chilies, add the lemon grass, ginger, garlic and shallots, then grind or process until smooth.

4 Add the shrimp paste, cilantro, mint or basil, nutmeg and vegetable oil to the food processor or mortar. Combine well.

5 Pour the coconut milk into a strainer. Pour the thin part of the milk, together with the chicken stock and the reserved mussel cooking liquid, into a wok. Reserve the coconut milk solids. Add 4–5 tablespoons of the green curry paste, according to taste. You can add more paste later, if you need to. Boil rapidly until the liquid has reduced completely.

6 Add the coconut milk solids, then add the squid and monkfish. Simmer for 15–20 minutes. Then add the shrimp, scallops and cooked mussels with the beans, bamboo shoots and tomato. Simmer for 2–3 minutes, transfer to a bowl and decorate with the basil and chilies. Serve with rice, if desired.

Shrimp Curry with Quails' Eggs

Quails' eggs are available at specialty stores and delicatessens. Hens' eggs may be substituted if quails' eggs are hard to find. Use 1 hen's egg to every 4 quails' eggs.

INGREDIENTS

Serves 4

12 quails' eggs

2 tablespoons vegetable oil

4 shallots or 1 medium onion, finely chopped

1-inch piece fresh ginger, finely chopped

2 garlic cloves, crushed

2-inch piece lemon grass, finely shredded

1–2 small, fresh red chilies, seeded and finely chopped

½ teaspoon turmeric

½-inch-square piece shrimp paste or 1 tablespoon fish sauce

2 pounds raw shrimp, peeled and deveined

1⅔ cups canned coconut milk

1¼ cups chicken stock

4 ounces spinach, roughly shredded

2 teaspoons sugar

½ teaspoon salt

2 scallions, green part only, shredded, and 2 tablespoons dry shredded coconut, to garnish

2 Heat the vegetable oil in a large wok, add the shallots, ginger and garlic and soften without coloring. Add the lemon grass, chilies, turmeric and shrimp paste and fry briefly to bring out their flavors.

3 Add the shrimp and fry briefly. Pour the coconut milk through a strainer over a bowl, then add the thin part of the milk with the chicken stock. Add the spinach, sugar and salt and bring to the boil. Simmer for 6–8 minutes.

4 Transfer to a serving dish, halve the quails' eggs and toss in the sauce. Scatter with the scallions and the shredded coconut and serve.

1 Cook the quails' eggs in boiling water for 8 minutes. Refresh in cold water, peel and then set aside.

PASTA,
NOODLE &
RICE DISHES

Spaghetti with Hot-and-sour Fish

A truly Chinese spicy taste is what
makes this sauce so different.

Serves 4

12 ounces spaghetti tricolore

1 pound monkfish, skinned

2 zucchini

1 fresh green chili, cored and seeded

1 tablespoon olive oil

1 large onion, chopped

1 teaspoon turmeric

1 cup peas, thawed if frozen

2 teaspoons lemon juice

5 tablespoons hoisin sauce

⅔ cup water

salt and freshly ground black pepper

dill sprig, to garnish

1 Cook the pasta in boiling salted water according to the instructions on the package, until tender, but still firm to the bite.

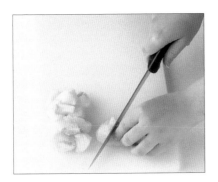

2 Meanwhile, with a large sharp knife, cut the monkfish into bite-size pieces.

COOK'S TIP

This dish is quite low in calories, so it is ideal for dieters. Hoisin sauce is widely available at most large supermarkets or Chinese food stores.

3 Thinly slice the zucchini, then finely chop the fresh, green chili. Set aside.

4 Heat the oil in a large frying pan and fry the onion for 5 minutes, until softened, but not colored. Add the turmeric.

5 Add the chili, zucchini and peas and fry over medium heat for about 5 minutes, until the vegetables have softened.

6 Stir in the fish, lemon juice, hoisin sauce and water. Bring to a boil, then simmer for about 5 minutes or until the fish is tender. Season to taste.

7 Drain the pasta thoroughly and transfer it to a serving bowl. Toss in the sauce to coat. Serve immediately, garnished with the fresh sprig of dill.

Tagliatelle with Smoked Salmon

This is a pretty pasta sauce that tastes as good as it looks. The light texture of the cucumber perfectly complements the fish. Different effects and color combinations can be achieved by using green, white or red tagliatelle—or even a mixture of all three.

INGREDIENTS

Serves 4

12 ounces dried or fresh tagliatelle

½ cucumber

6 tablespoons (¾ stick) butter

grated rind of 1 orange

2 tablespoons chopped fresh dill

1¼ cups light cream or half-and-half

1 tablespoon orange juice

4 ounces smoked salmon, skinned

salt and freshly ground black pepper

1 If using dried pasta, cook in lightly salted boiling water following the manufacturer's instructions on the package. If using fresh pasta, cook in lightly salted boiling water for 2–3 minutes or until just tender but still firm to the bite.

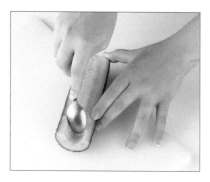

2 Using a sharp knife, cut the cucumber in half lengthwise. Using a small spoon, scoop out the cucumber seeds and discard.

3 Turn the cucumber halves onto their flat sides and slice thinly.

4 Melt the butter in a heavy saucepan, add the grated orange rind and fresh dill and stir well. Add the cucumber and cook gently over low heat for about 2 minutes, stirring occasionally.

5 Add the cream, orange juice and seasoning to taste and simmer gently for 1 minute.

6 Meanwhile, cut the salmon into thin strips.

7 Stir the salmon into the sauce and heat through.

8 Drain the pasta thoroughly and toss it in the sauce. Serve immediately.

COOK'S TIP

A more economical way to make this special-occasion sauce is to use smoked salmon pieces, sold relatively inexpensively at most delicatessens and some super-markets. (These are just scraps and awkwardly shaped pieces that are unsuitable for recipes requiring whole slices of smoked salmon.) Smoked trout is a less expensive alternative, but it lacks the rich flavor and color of smoked salmon.

Black Pasta with Squid Sauce

Tagliatelle flavored with squid ink looks amazing and tastes deliciously of the sea. You'll find it at good Italian delicatessens.

INGREDIENTS

Serves 4

½ cup olive oil

2 shallots, chopped

2 garlic cloves, crushed

3 tablespoons chopped fresh parsley

1½ pounds cleaned squid, cut into rings and rinsed

⅔ cup dry white wine

1 can (14 ounces) chopped tomatoes

½ teaspoon dried chili flakes or powder

1 pound black tagliatelle

salt and freshly ground black pepper

1 Heat the oil in a pan and add the shallots. Cook until pale golden in color, then add the garlic. When the garlic colors a little, add 2 tablespoons of the parsley, stir, then add the squid and stir again. Cook for 3–4 minutes, then add the wine.

2 Simmer for a few seconds, then add the tomatoes and chili flakes or powder and season with salt and pepper to taste. Cover and simmer gently for about 1 hour, until the squid is tender. Add more water if necessary.

3 Cook the pasta in plenty of boiling salted water, according to the instructions on the package, until tender, but still firm to the bite. Drain and return the pasta to the pan. Add the squid sauce and mix well. Sprinkle each serving with the remaining chopped parsley and serve immediately.

COOK'S TIP

The labeling of olive oil can be confusing. The oil is basically divided into two types—pure and virgin. The latter comes from the first pressing, but virgin olive oil is further sub-divided, according to its level of acidity. The least acidic and therefore the best oil is extra virgin. Use this quality for special dishes and salad dressings, but the next best oil—virgin— may be used for general cooking. Pure olive oil, although not in any way adulterated, lacks the unique flavor of virgin oil.

Pasta with Scallops in Tomato Sauce

Delicate and simple, this pasta dish makes a good appetizer or main dish.

INGREDIENTS

Serves 4

1 pound long, thin pasta, such as fettucine
   or linguine
2 tablespoons olive oil
2 garlic cloves, finely chopped
1 pound prepared scallops, sliced in
   half horizontally
2 tablespoons chopped fresh basil
salt and freshly ground black pepper
fresh basil sprigs, to garnish

For the sauce
2 tablespoons olive oil
½ onion, finely chopped
1 garlic clove, finely chopped
2 cans (14 ounces each) peeled
   tomatoes

1 To make the sauce, heat the oil in a non-stick frying pan. Add the onion, garlic and a little salt, and cook for about 5 minutes, stirring occasionally, until just softened, but not colored.

2 Add the tomatoes with their juice, and crush with a fork. Bring to a boil, then lower the heat and simmer gently for 15 minutes. Remove the pan from the heat and set aside.

3 Bring a large pan of salted water to a boil. Add the pasta and cook until just tender to the bite, according to the instructions on the package.

4 Meanwhile, combine the oil and garlic in another non-stick frying pan and cook for about 30 seconds, until just sizzling. Add the scallops and ½ teaspoon salt and cook over high heat for about 3 minutes, tossing, until the scallops are cooked completely through.

5 Add the scallops to the tomato sauce. Season with salt and pepper to taste, then stir gently and keep warm.

6 Drain the pasta and rinse under hot water. Add the scallop sauce and the basil and toss thoroughly. Serve immediately, garnished with fresh basil sprigs.

Baked Seafood Spaghetti

In this dish, each portion is baked and served in an individual parcel, which is then opened at the table. Use parchment paper or aluminum foil to make the parcels.

INGREDIENTS

Serves 4

1 pound fresh mussels

½ cup dry white wine

¼ cup olive oil

2 garlic cloves, finely chopped

1 pound tomatoes, fresh or canned, peeled and finely chopped

14 ounces spaghetti or other long pasta

8 ounces fresh, or frozen and thawed, uncooked peeled shrimp, deveined

2 tablespoons chopped fresh parsley

salt and freshly ground black pepper

1 Scrub the mussels well under cold running water, cutting off the beards with a small sharp knife. Discard any with broken shells or that do not close immediately when sharply tapped. Place the mussels and the wine in a large saucepan and heat until they open.

2 Lift out the mussels and remove to a side dish. Discard any that do not open. Strain the cooking liquid through clean muslin to remove any grit and reserve until needed.

3 In a medium saucepan, heat the oil and garlic together for 1–2 minutes. Add the tomatoes, and cook over medium to high heat until they soften. Stir in ¾ cup of the reserved cooking liquid from the mussels and simmer gently.

4 Meanwhile, cook the pasta in a large pan of boiling salted water, according to the package instructions, until tender, but still firm to the bite.

5 Just before draining the pasta, add the shrimp and parsley to the tomato sauce. Simmer for another 2 minutes or until the shrimp are cooked through. Taste and adjust the seasoning, if necessary. Remove from the heat and set aside. Drain the pasta.

6 Prepare 4 pieces of parchment paper approximately 12 x 18 inches in size. Place each sheet in the center of a shallow bowl. Transfer the drained pasta to a mixing bowl. Add the tomato sauce and mix well. Stir in the mussels.

7 Divide the pasta and seafood between the 4 pieces of paper, placing a mound in the center of each and twisting the paper ends together to make a closed packet. (The bowl under the paper will prevent the sauce from spilling while the paper parcels are being closed.) Arrange on a large baking sheet and bake at 300°F for 8–10 minutes. Place an unopened packet on each of 4 individual serving plates.

Seafood Laska

For a special occasion serve creamy rice noodles in a spicy, coconut-flavored broth, topped with a selection of seafood. There is a fair amount of work involved in the preparation, but you can make the soup base ahead.

INGREDIENTS

Serves 4

4 fresh red chilies, seeded and
   roughly chopped
1 onion, roughly chopped
1 piece balachan, the size of a stock cube
1 lemon grass stalk, chopped
1 small piece fresh ginger, roughly
   chopped
6 macadamia nuts or almonds
¼ cup vegetable oil
1 teaspoon paprika
1 teaspoon ground turmeric
2 cups stock or water
2½ cups coconut milk
fish sauce (see method)
12 raw jumbo shrimp, peeled and
   deveined
8 scallops
8 ounces prepared squid, cut into rings
12 ounces rice vermicelli or rice noodles,
   soaked in warm water until soft
salt and freshly ground black pepper
lime halves, to serve

For the garnish
¼ cucumber, cut into matchsticks
2 fresh red chilies, seeded and
   finely sliced
2 tablespoons mint leaves
2 tablespoons fried shallots

COOK'S TIP

Balachan is dried shrimp or shrimp paste. It is sold in small blocks, and you will find it at Asian supermarkets.

1 In a blender or food processor, process the chilies, onion, balachan, lemon grass, ginger and nuts until smooth in texture.

2 Heat 3 tablespoons of the oil in a large saucepan. Add the chili paste and fry for 6 minutes. Stir in the paprika and turmeric and fry for about 2 minutes more.

3 Add the stock and the coconut milk to the pan. Bring to a boil, reduce the heat and simmer gently for 15–20 minutes. Season to taste with the fish sauce.

4 Season the seafood with salt and pepper. Heat the remaining oil in a frying pan, add the seafood and stir-fry quickly for 2–3 minutes until cooked.

5 Add the noodles to the broth and heat through. Divide among individual serving bowls. Place the fried seafood on top, then garnish with the cucumber, chilies, mint and fried shallots. Serve with the limes.

Bamie Goreng

This fried noodle dish from Indonesia is wonderfully accommodating. To the basic recipe you can add other vegetables, such as mushrooms, broccoli, leeks or bean sprouts. You can use whatever you have on hand, bearing in mind the importance of achieving a balance of colors, flavors and textures.

INGREDIENTS

Serves 6–8

1 pound dried egg noodles

1 boneless skinless chicken breast

4 ounces pork fillet

4 ounces calves' liver (optional)

2 eggs, beaten

6 tablespoons oil

2 tablespoons butter or margarine

2 garlic cloves, crushed

4 ounces cooked peeled large shrimp

4 ounces spinach

2 celery stalks, finely sliced

4 scallions, shredded

about ¼ cup chicken stock

dark soy sauce and light soy sauce

salt and freshly ground black pepper

deep-fried onions and celery leaves,
  to garnish

mixed fruit and vegetable salad, to
  serve (optional)

1 Cook the noodles in lightly salted boiling water for 3–4 minutes. Drain, rinse with cold water and drain well again. Set aside until needed.

2 Finely slice the chicken, pork fillet and calves' liver, if using.

3 Season the eggs. Heat 1 teaspoon of the oil with the butter in a small pan until melted. Stir in the eggs and keep stirring until scrambled. Set aside.

4 Heat the remaining oil in a preheated wok and stir-fry the garlic with the chicken, pork and liver for 2–3 minutes, until they have changed color. Stir in the shrimp, spinach, celery and scallions, and mix well.

5 Add the drained noodles and toss the mixture well so that all the ingredients are thoroughly combined. Add just enough stock to moisten and add dark and light soy sauce to taste. Finally, stir in the scrambled eggs.

6 Garnish the dish with deep-fried onions and celery leaves. Serve with a mixed fruit and vegetable salad, if desired.

Seafood Chow Mein

This basic recipe can be adapted using a range of different items for the "'dressing."

Serves 4

3 ounces squid, cleaned

3 ounces raw shrimp

3–4 fresh scallops, prepared

½ egg white

1 tablespoon cornstarch paste

8 ounces egg noodles

5–6 tablespoons vegetable oil

2 ounces snow peas

½ teaspoon salt

½ teaspoon light brown sugar

1 tablespoon Chinese rice wine or
   dry sherry

2 tablespoons light soy sauce

2 scallions, finely shredded

vegetable or chicken stock, if necessary

few drops sesame oil

1 Open up the squid and, using a sharp knife, score the inside in a crisscross pattern. Cut the squid into pieces, each about the size of a postage stamp. Soak the squid in a bowl of boiling water until all the pieces curl up. Rinse in cold water and drain.

2 Peel and devein the shrimp, then cut each of them in half lengthwise.

3 Cut each scallop into 3–4 slices. Mix the scallops and shrimp with the egg white and cornstarch paste and set aside.

4 Cook the noodles in boiling water according to the package instructions, then drain and rinse under cold water. Mix with about 1 tablespoon of the oil.

5 Heat 2–3 tablespoons of the oil in a preheated wok until hot. Stir-fry the snow peas and seafood for about 2 minutes, then add the salt, sugar, rice wine or sherry, half of the soy sauce and about half of the scallions. Blend well and add a little stock, if necessary. Remove and keep warm.

6 Heat the remaining oil in the wok and stir-fry the noodles for 2–3 minutes with the remaining soy sauce. Place in a large serving dish, pour the "dressing" on top, garnish with the remaining scallions and sprinkle with sesame oil. Serve hot or cold.

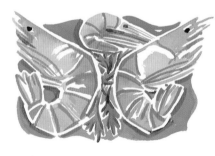

COOK'S TIP

To make cornstarch paste, mix 4 parts dry cornstarch with about 5 parts cold water until smooth.

Buckwheat Noodles with Smoked Trout

The light, crisp texture of the bok choy balances the strong, earthy flavors of the mushrooms and the smokiness of the trout.

INGREDIENTS

Serves 4

12 ounces buckwheat noodles

2 tablespoons vegetable oil

4 ounces fresh shiitake mushrooms, quartered

2 garlic cloves, finely chopped

1 tablespoon grated fresh ginger

8 ounces bok choy

1 scallion, finely sliced diagonally

1 tablespoon dark sesame oil

2 tablespoons mirin

2 tablespoons soy sauce

2 smoked trout, skinned and boned

salt and freshly ground black pepper

2 tablespoons cilantro leaves and 2 teaspoons sesame seeds, toasted, to garnish

1 Cook the buckwheat noodles in a saucepan of boiling water for 7–10 minutes, or until just tender, according to the instructions on the package.

2 Meanwhile, heat the oil in a large frying pan. Add the shiitake mushrooms and sauté over medium heat for 3 minutes. Add the garlic, ginger and bok choy, and continue to sauté for another 2 minutes.

3 Drain the noodles and add them to the mushroom mixture, with the scallion, sesame oil, mirin and soy sauce. Toss and season with salt and pepper to taste.

4 Break up the trout into bite-size pieces. Arrange the noodle mixture on individual serving plates and top with trout.

5 Garnish the noodles with cilantro leaves and sesame seeds and serve immediately.

COOK'S TIP
↬

Mirin is sweet, cooking sake, available at Japanese stores.

Stir-fried Noodles with Sweet Salmon

A delicious sauce forms the marinade for the salmon in this recipe. Served with soft-fried noodles, it makes a stunning dish.

INGREDIENTS

Serves 4

350g/12oz salmon fillet

30ml/2 tbsp Japanese soy sauce (shoyu)

30ml/2 tbsp sake

60ml/4 tbsp mirin or sweet sherry

5ml/1 tsp light brown soft sugar

10ml/2 tsp grated fresh root ginger

3 cloves garlic, 1 crushed, and 2 sliced into rounds

30ml/2 tbsp groundnut oil

225g/8oz dried egg noodles, cooked and drained

50g/2oz alfalfa sprouts

30ml/2 tbsp sesame seeds, lightly toasted

1 Thinly slice the salmon, then place in a shallow dish.

2 In a bowl, mix together the soy sauce, sake, mirin or sherry, sugar, ginger and crushed garlic. Pour over the salmon, cover and leave to marinate for 30 minutes.

3 Drain the salmon, scraping off and reserving the marinade. Place the salmon in a single layer on a baking sheet. Cook under a preheated grill for 2–3 minutes, without turning.

4 Meanwhile, heat a wok until hot, add the oil and swirl it around. Add the garlic rounds and cook until golden brown, but do not allow them to burn.

5 Add the cooked noodles and reserved marinade to the wok. Stir-fry for 3–4 minutes, until the marinade has reduced slightly to make a syrupy glaze that coats the egg noodles.

6 Toss in the alfalfa sprouts, then remove immediately from the heat. Transfer to warmed serving plates and top with the salmon. Sprinkle over the toasted sesame seeds. Serve at once.

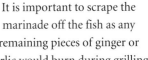

COOK'S TIP

It is important to scrape the marinade off the fish as any remaining pieces of ginger or garlic would burn during grilling and spoil the finished dish.

Salmon Risotto

Any rice can be used for risotto, although the creamiest ones are made with short grain arborio rice. Fresh tarragon and cucumber combine well to bring out the flavor of the salmon.

INGREDIENTS

Serves 4

2 tablespoons butter

1 small bunch scallions, white part only, chopped

½ cucumber, peeled, seeded and chopped

14 ounces short grain arborio rice

4 cups chicken or fish stock

⅔ cup dry white wine

1 pound salmon fillet, skinned and diced

3 tablespoons chopped fresh tarragon

1 Heat the butter in a large saucepan and add the scallions and cucumber. Cook for 2–3 minutes without coloring.

2 Add the rice, chicken stock and wine, bring to a boil and simmer, uncovered, for 10 minutes, stirring occasionally.

3 Stir in the diced salmon and chopped tarragon. Continue cooking for another 5 minutes, then switch off the heat. Cover the pan and let stand for 5 minutes before serving.

VARIATION

Long grain rice can also be used. Choose grains that have not been precooked and reduce the stock to 3 cups per 14 ounces of rice.

Fish with Rice

This Arabic fish dish, Sayadieh, is very popular in the Lebanon.

Serves 4–6
juice of 1 lemon
3 tablespoons oil
2 pounds cod steaks
4 large onions, chopped
1 teaspoon ground cumin
2–3 saffron strands, soaked in
  2 tablespoons hot water
4 cups fish stock
1¼ pounds basmati or long grain rice
4 ounces pine nuts, lightly toasted
salt and freshly ground black pepper
fresh parsley, to garnish

1 Combine the lemon juice and 1 tablespoon of the oil in a shallow dish. Add the fish steaks, turning to coat, then cover and set aside to marinate for 30 minutes.

2 Heat the remaining oil in a large saucepan or flameproof casserole and fry the onions for 5–6 minutes, until softened and golden, stirring occasionally.

3 Drain the fish, reserving the marinade, and add to the pan. Fry for 1–2 minutes on each side until lightly golden, then add the cumin, saffron strands and a little salt and pepper.

4 Pour in the fish stock and the reserved marinade, bring to a boil and then simmer very gently, over low heat, for 5–10 minutes, until the fish is nearly done.

5 Transfer the fish to a plate and add the rice to the stock. Bring to a boil, then reduce the heat and simmer very gently over low heat for 15 minutes, until nearly all the stock has been absorbed.

6 Arrange the fish on the rice and cover. Steam over low heat for another 15–20 minutes.

7 Transfer the fish to a plate, then spoon the rice onto a large flat dish and arrange the fish on top. Sprinkle with lightly toasted pine nuts and garnish with fresh parsley.

COOK'S TIP

Take care when cooking the rice that the saucepan does not boil dry. Check it occasionally and add more stock or water, if it becomes necessary.

Mixed Fish Jambalaya

Jambalaya, from New Orleans, is not unlike a paella, but much spicier. The name comes from the French word "jambon," and tells us that the dish was originally based on ham, but you can add many other ingredients of your choice, including fish and shellfish.

INGREDIENTS

Serves 4

2 tablespoons oil

6–8 strips bacon, diced

1 onion, chopped

2 stalks celery, chopped

2 large garlic cloves, chopped

1 teaspoon cayenne pepper

2 bay leaves

1 teaspoon dried oregano

½ teaspoon dried thyme

4 medium tomatoes, skinned, seeded
   and chopped

⅔ cup ready-made tomato sauce

12 ounces long grain rice

2 cups fish stock

6 ounces firm white fish (cod or haddock),
   skinned, boned and cubed

4 ounces cooked peeled shrimp

salt and freshly ground black pepper

2 chopped scallions, to garnish

1 Heat the oil in a large saucepan and fry the bacon until crisp. Add the onion and celery and stir until they begin to stick to the base of the pan.

2 Add the garlic, cayenne pepper, herbs, tomatoes and seasoning and mix well. Stir in the tomato sauce, rice and stock and bring to a boil.

3 Gently stir in the fish and transfer to an ovenproof dish. Cover tightly with foil and bake at 350°F for 20–30 minutes, until the rice is just tender. Stir in the shrimp and heat through. Serve sprinkled with the scallions.

Spanish Seafood Paella

Paella is also the name of the heavy, cast-iron pan in which this dish is traditionally cooked.

INGREDIENTS

Serves 4

¼ cup olive oil

8 ounces monkfish or cod, skinned and
    cut into chunks

3 prepared baby squid, bodies cut into
    rings and tentacles chopped

1 red mullet, filleted, skinned and cut into
    chunks (optional)

1 onion, chopped

3 garlic cloves, finely chopped

1 red bell pepper, seeded and sliced

4 tomatoes, skinned and chopped

8 ounces arborio rice

2 cups fish stock

⅔ cup white wine

½ cup frozen peas

4–5 saffron strands soaked in
    2 tablespoons hot water

4 ounces cooked peeled shrimp

8 fresh mussels in shells, scrubbed

salt and freshly ground black pepper

1 tablespoon chopped fresh parsley,
    to garnish

lemon wedges, to serve

1 Heat 2 tablespoons of the olive oil in a large frying pan and add the monkfish, the squid and the red mullet, if using. Stir-fry for 2 minutes, then transfer the fish to a bowl with all the juices and set aside.

2 Heat the remaining 2 tablespoons of oil in the pan and add the onion, garlic and red pepper. Fry for 6–7 minutes, stirring frequently, until the onion and pepper have softened.

3 Stir in the tomatoes and fry for 2 minutes, then add the rice, stirring to coat the grains with oil, and cook for 2–3 minutes. Pour on the fish stock and wine and add the peas, saffron and water. Season well and mix.

4 Gently stir in the fish with all the juices, followed by the shrimp, and then push the mussels into the rice. Cover and cook over low heat for about 30 minutes, or until the stock has been absorbed but the mixture is still moist.

5 Remove from the heat, keep covered and let stand for 5 minutes. Discard any mussels that do not open. Sprinkle the paella with parsley and serve with lemon wedges.

Index